Praise for *The Enchanted Earth*

"Maureen Calamia has given us a fine addition to the growing literature on nature connection. Readers will see themselves in this passionate and compassionate book."

—**Richard Louv,** author of *Last Child in the Woods*, *Vitamin N*, and other books about the human-nature connection

"One of the biggest shifts in my life occurred when I realized that every tree is my brother, every cloud my sister. Even the ornery squirrels who cleverly thwart my every attempt to keep them out of my bird feeder will forever be part of me. I am grateful for this book and the growing re-remembering that every living being is sacred and indeed enchanted."

—**Pam Grout,** #1 *New York Times* bestselling author of twenty-one books

"This is a book that will make you pause, reflect, and wonder! From enchanted forests and glorious skies to magical animals, the book takes you on a journey to rediscover and heal your own life through nature and the everyday miracles we see and take for granted."

—**Sumita Singha,** educator, researcher, and founder of Ecologic Architects

"This heartfelt compilation calls us back to what is most precious and fundamental to this human journey—our relationship with the Earth. It inspires us to dissolve fear and separateness by reconnecting with the living world around us, remembering that we are one with nature and life's intrinsic goodness. There is magic within these pages..."

—**Llyn "Cedar" Roberts,** MA, award-winning author and spiritual ecologist

"This book is more than an honorable tribute to Earth. It's a message of hope, giving voice to the unheard anecdotes, to the sometimes abandoned or almost forgotten experiences that each of the storytellers, including the author, shares. Simultaneously, *The Enchanted Earth* lends the reader an intimate space to reflect on her own experiences and subtleties with nature. Maureen Calamia weaves a luminous contribution to humanity with her love for nature through the collections of stories in *The Enchanted Earth*. Each recollection is captivating and told with sensible, raw emotion, connecting the reader to something deeply moving and nostalgic. This book is a message of hope and reminds us that the Earth feels and is deeply connected to each of us."

—**Patsy Balacchi**, feng shui and brand consultant

"Maureen K. Calamia's *The Enchanted Earth* studies how nature alters our lives by linking our inner and outer landscapes. Her insights inspire a deeper bond and a relational shift with the natural world. A must-read book that offers valuable guidance for harmonizing our inner selves with the environment for the planet's survival and our own."

—**Itzhak Beery**, leading ancestral medicine teacher, healer, speaker, and author of *The Gift of Shamanism*, *Shamanic Transformations*, and *Shamanic Healing*

"Scientists, therapists, marketing people, politicians, and shamans know that when we change our perceptions, we change our actions and that changes reality—for us as individuals and for communities at large. Maureen's book addresses this issue eloquently and guides us along the path of a global consciousness change that can lead us back from the precipice of disaster to a world where future generations of all species can thrive."

—**John Perkins**, *New York Times* bestselling author of *Confessions of an Economic Hit Man*

"I absolutely adored this book—it's so timely and resonant! As you dive in, you'll hear from forest and wildlife experts, depth psychologists, philosophers, earth-based practitioners, and more. Each voice weaves together a beautiful tapestry of personal experiences: stunning landscapes, unique weather, the warm embrace of trees and plants, and magical encounters with wildlife. Reading *The Enchanted Earth* felt like embarking on a personal journey of discovery and transformation, leaving me feeling deeply connected to the natural world."

—**Dr. Kim Hermanson,** award-winning author, visionary creative consultant, and founder of the MetaphorMind revolution

"The binding call for reciprocal and responsible ecological relations is a collective one. In visceral response to the pressing issues of our time, Maureen entangled her sensible wisdom with other voices and geographies, bringing rich and diverse accounts of relations to place, each offering a unique perspective. All these embodied stories were carefully threaded together by Maureen's tender insights."

—**Sofia Batalha,** teacher and author of *Underground Mysteries of Iberian Myth*

"Maureen Calamia summons the magic of our encounters with the natural world, revealing through a variety of perspectives how we can reenter through enchantment the earthly Great Conversation around us that includes the more-than-human."

—**Craig Chalquist**, PhD

"I have dedicated my life to reconnecting people with nature through my treehouses. It is my passion! *The Enchanted Earth* is Maureen's beautiful work of doing the same—helping people rekindle the magic of the natural world through our stories. In sharing my story, it helped me relive the experience of deep nature connection. You will love this enchanting book!"

—**Pete Nelson,** host of *Treehouse Masters*

"Maureen Calamia spent years interviewing a unique assortment of experts on how the natural world transforms us, from grief and other rites of passage to spiritual beliefs. The book's diverse voices range from park rangers and nature guides to earth-friendly designers and architects, from philosophers and psychotherapists to CEOs, from treehouse builders and earth-based practitioners to celebrities, from journalists to shamans and the occasional Buddhist nun. Calamia's interdisciplinary storytelling approach implements what climate activists are finally beginning to understand—that any solution requires changing the narrative around what we tell ourselves about the planet and our relationship to it. The more than forty people Calamia interviewed reveal connections to nature that are profound and surprising, often even to themselves. Scattered throughout the conversational text are 'invitations' or experiential prompts for encountering nature. The result is both an urgent love letter to our dying earth and a celebratory handbook for living and healing."

—**Faith Adiele,** author of *Meeting Faith: The Thai Forest Journals of a Black Buddhist Nun* and *Travel Writing Will Save the World: A Guide for Transforming Ourselves & Others*

"The beautiful book shares stories of nature-connection which are essential to the experience of being human—and offers ways for us to deepen our relations to the Earth. The stories so heartfully share a sense of compassion, affection, and love for our planet. In *The Enchanted Earth*, Maureen has thoughtfully gathered some of these amazing stories, weaving them together in a way that is inspiring and thought-provoking. I truly appreciate this work, which will open pathways for others in our quest for belonging—and help us uncover the many conscious ways we can help to heal ourselves while healing the planet."

—**Sonja Bochart,** regenerative practitioner

"Maureen Calamia writes from the heart, sharing her story and the stories of others, reminding us of what is sacred in the natural world. With language that is inspiring, luminous, and accessible, she reveals the power of the stories we experience, share, and tell others. Encouraging us to breathe life into our own connection with the earth, she lays out a path to recovering the connection to what is divine and sacred within ourselves. She is lighting the way for all of us."

—**Lisa Kahn,** CEO, founder of Finding Sanctuary

"In *The Enchanted Earth*, Maureen Calamia has woven together stories of human and interspecies connection that uplift our souls. A truly inspiring book filled with awe, beauty, and profound meaning. Read—and be transformed!"

—**Nicole Craanen,** MFA, NCIDQ, WELL-AP, LEED Green-Associate, ANFT, and founder of the Biophilic Design Institute

"I highly recommend *The Enchanted Earth* by Maureen Calamia, where diverse people's immersive nature experiences are explored. Each page is filled with inspiring and captivating stories sharing the interwoven relationship between nature and the human spirit. I highly recommend this book to anyone, especially those of us seeking to deepen our reconnection with Earth's love and sacred wisdom."

—**Bonnie Casamassima,** researcher and founder, Intuitive By Nature

"*The Enchanted Earth* shares stories of deep connection with nature, stories that remind us that we are in conversation and communion with the world around us. At this critical junction in human evolution, when it is more important than ever to find our way back to balance, *The Enchanted Earth* provides a path—not for the intellect—but for the heart."

—**Maia Toll,** award-winning author

The
Enchanted Earth

Also by Maureen Calamia

Creating Luminous Spaces: Use the Five Elements for Balance and Harmony in Your Home and in Your Life (Conari Press, 2018)

The Enchanted Earth

*Embracing the Power of Nature
to Discover the Wild in You*

by

Maureen Calamia

MIAMI

Copyright © 2024 by Maureen K. Calamia.
Published by Mango Publishing, a division of Mango Publishing Group, Inc.

Cover, Layout & Design: Megan Werner
Cover Photo: Michael / stock.adobe.com

Mango is an active supporter of authors' rights to free speech and artistic expression in their books. The purpose of copyright is to encourage authors to produce exceptional works that enrich our culture and our open society.

Uploading or distributing photos, scans or any content from this book without prior permission is theft of the author's intellectual property. Please honor the author's work as you would your own. Thank you in advance for respecting our author's rights.

For permission requests, please contact the publisher at:
Mango Publishing Group
5966 South Dixie Highway, Suite 300
Miami, FL 33143
info@mango.bz

For special orders, quantity sales, course adoptions and corporate sales, please email the publisher at sales@mango.bz. For trade and wholesale sales, please contact Ingram Publisher Services at customer.service@ingramcontent.com or +1.800.509.4887.

The Enchanted Earth: Embracing the Power of Nature to Discover the Wild in You

Library of Congress Cataloging-in-Publication number: 2024943899
ISBN: (p) 978-1-68481-685-9 (e) 978-1-68481-686-6
BISAC category code OCC033000, BODY, MIND & SPIRIT / Gaia & Earth Energies

From *The Wild Edge of Sorrow: Rituals of Renewal and the Sacred Work of Grief* by Francis Weller, published by North Atlantic Books, copyright © 2015 by Francis Weller. Reprinted by permission of North Atlantic Books.

The information provided in this book is based on the research, insights, and experiences of the author. Every effort has been made to provide accurate and up-to-date information; however, neither the author nor the publisher warrants the information provided is free of factual error. This book is not intended to diagnose, treat, or cure any medical condition or disease, nor is it intended as a substitute for professional medical care. All matters regarding your health should be supervised by a qualified healthcare professional. The author and publisher disclaim all liability for any adverse effects arising out of or relating to the use or application of the information or advice provided in this book.

To Joe, Allison, Bobby, Nicole, and Pat.
May you always find the joy of nature
around and within you.

"We were not meant to live shallow lives, pocked by meaningless routines and the secondary satisfactions of happy hour. We are the inheritors of an amazing lineage, rippling with memories of life lived intimately with bison and gazelle, raven and the night sky. We are designed to encounter this life with amazement and wonder, not resignation and endurance. This is at the very heart of our grief and sorrow. The dream of full-throated living, woven into our very being, has often been forgotten and neglected, replaced by a societal fiction of productivity and material gain. No wonder we seek distractions. Every sorrow we carry extends from the absence of what we require to stay engaged in this one wild and precious life."

—Francis Weller

Table of Contents

Foreword	14
Introduction	16
Chapter 1: The Urgent Call	30
Chapter 2: How Nature Speaks to Us	50
Chapter 3: Heart-Opening Awe, Oneness & Grief	70
Chapter 4:: Invitations to Connect with Trees	93
Chapter 5: Close Encounters with the Wild	122
Chapter 6: Weather, Cosmos, and Natural Phenomena	145
Chapter 7: Synchronistic Life Path Nudges	169
Chapter 8: Rites of Passage	190
Chapter 9: The "Super" Natural in Waking Life	209
Chapter 10: What's Your Story?	238
Appendix	252
Acknowledgments	266
About the Author	269

Foreword

In these chaotic times, we face a wasteland—a metaphor that runs deep in our subconscious. This wasteland reflects our inner worlds, a mirror of the degradation within our hearts and souls as we witness injustices against humanity and all living beings.

The overwhelming stress and despair for our planet have reached a fever pitch. Yet, for some of us, there is a different perspective. We recognize the cycles and seasons of death and rebirth, the breakdown that leads to breakthrough.

We are living through what ecologist Joanna Macy calls "The Great Turning"—a period of immense chaos. But, just as the chrysalis stage appears anarchic to the caterpillar, it is a necessary state on the path to transformation.

Many of us who walk this path see a new mythology arising—one for individual souls, the collective, and the planet itself. The old stories no longer fit these accelerating, transitional times.

To write this new mythology, we need stories of heart-based wonder, awe, and mystery. We must summon our individual experiences with the natural world, both remembered and forgotten.

The images and metaphors within our stories shape us, often unconsciously. But when we find the right words to express what we know deeply, those symbols, rich with meaning, can empower us to uncover our new myths.

I met Maureen when she approached me for an interview while writing this book. She wanted to hear one of my stories, and something about her request moved me to agree.

I spontaneously shared a story that may be one of the foundational myths of my life: as a child at summer camp, I gazed at the immense night sky and, in that moment, I felt a deep desire to explore the great mystery of consciousness.

I found Maureen's earnest desire to share these important stories of profound connection very timely. Although our conversation was two years ago, her project feels more urgent now than ever before. We need to harness the power of our stories to co-create this new mythology.

These stories, through their metaphors and symbols, impart magic and meaning. They reawaken sacred experiences long dormant within us, allowing us to see our authentic selves reflected back, perhaps for the first time.

We need these stories—to share, to listen, to reflect on our deepest bonds with the Earth, the Universe, and everything in between. I hope you read this treasured book with an open heart, and listen for the stories that want to be acknowledged, contemplated, and integrated into your life, your new mythology.

For this is indeed, an enchanted Earth.

Jean Shinoda Bolen,
9/10/24

Introduction

"I'm talking about not covering every square inch with houses and strip malls, until you can't remember what happens when you stand in a meadow at dusk."

"What happens in the meadow at dusk?"

"Nothing!"

"Everything!"

"Nothing!"

"Everything!"

"Nothing!"

"Everything!"
"It's beautiful..."

—I Heart Huckabees
Dialogue between an environmental activist and
a family with fundamentalist religious values.

There are certain moments in our lives that stand out from the rest. A specific sunset among the 25,000 or more we experience in our lives. A look from a doe crossing the road in the moonlight. A gentle breeze timed perfectly to quell our depressive thoughts. The embrace of a tree, providing both comfort and guidance. Nature has a way of elevating the mundane and helping us feel more present.

These experiences are the ones that we not only recall, but treasure, when we are feeling ungrounded, hopeless, and confused. We remember what we were doing, what we were thinking, and how we responded. We can recall the quality of natural light, the scents, the temperature, perhaps even what we were wearing. These moments may have occurred decades ago, but they remain as vivid in our minds as if they happened yesterday.

If each of us wrote our autobiographies, these experiences would certainly make it to those pages in some form. They are the moments that helped shape our perspective about a relationship or situation—perhaps serving as a catalyst to a new calling or changing our lives in some way.

At least that is what I thought.

Yes, there were some people that, when asked to discuss a profound nature experience, would immediately recount a story (or several) that profoundly shifted them in some way, even subtly. Some even say that there are "so many stories, it's hard to pick one!"

But with others, my request was met with confusion. The response came in the form of another question. "What do you mean by 'profound?' "

A profound nature experience. What I really meant was an experience that challenged their current philosophical worldview. Life-altering. A time that enabled them to feel, or truly witness, the sacred within nature. And these experiences could have such a subtle shift that no one else would notice.

An experience that opened the door to an enchanted Earth.

Since the contributors to this book are a tiny subset of the general population—namely, people that are involved with nature somehow in their careers—I would have thought that they would all have lots to share.

The contributors include park rangers, authors of nature-based books, professors, philosophers, travel journalists and photographers, filmmakers, biophilic architects and consultants, earth-based practitioners, and shamans, among others. Not to mention, they also agreed to participate after receiving an email to help them prepare. So I was surprised that some of them seemed to struggle for a story.

Because I am eternally curious, I find myself asking people that I encounter in my everyday life about an experience they could share.

One of the most common stories I heard was an unusual encounter with wildlife, which they described to be a message from the spirit of a loved one that died. I heard about butterflies, dragonflies, and cardinals who showed up after a loved one had recently passed, sometimes even continuing to appear at key moments, bringing with them a message of peace.

These experiences are helpful and magical, in that they offer comfort and connection, but are they profound?

Many people seemed to be at a loss; they could not think of anything to share.

My amateur research confirms the importance of this book.

In my first book, *Creating Luminous Spaces*, I recounted one of my memories in nature, as an adult on a beach in Maui. It subtly shifted my understanding of reality.

But I realized that, before writing about this topic, it was difficult for even me to recount a profound story of my own. I realized that our stories need to be remembered, have life breathed back into them. They need to be alive in our hearts, perhaps written down in a journal, and even shared with others. Sure, I've had many moments of witnessing beauty and peace. But were those moments life-altering?

When we don't allow these experiences to see the light of day, they will not flower. But I've learned that those moments are not lost forever. They are still in us and can be awakened like the cicada from its wintertime slumber. They can be awakened through remembrance and contemplation.

Houston, we have a problem.

The quote at the beginning of this chapter, from the 2004 movie *I Heart Huckabees*, shockingly demonstrates the split between dogmatic religion and our experience of nature. How can we not see the Divine in all of creation?

With our focus on the science of nature, so little remains sacred. Most discoveries seem to demonstrate that everything can be explained by the mechanization of the Universe. What cannot be explained is cast aside as an aberration or mathematical error.

One alarming statistic is that we, the American population (and much of the developed world), spend at least 90 percent of our time indoors. Most of us do not work in the outdoors nor are we exposed to the elements of nature on a regular basis.

In contrast, many experts are starting to understand the issues around humanity's rapid disconnection from the rhythms of the natural world. We are part of nature and have been completely dependent upon nature for our survival for millions of years. But with increased technology, we have the audacity to act so independently from nature that we now build mega cities in the desert.

Journalist Richard Louv, in his 2005 book, *The Last Child in the Woods*, brought the issues of disconnection among our children. He coined the term nature-deficit disorder (NDD) to describe the separation of today's youth from the outdoors and laid out the facts. He reached the conclusion that NDD is highly correlated to the alarming rise of childhood diseases, diabetes and obesity, mental illness, and other societal challenges such as ADHD (attention deficit hyperactive disorder), as well as increased rates of depression and suicide.

Louv said, in essence, that technology is helpful and desired, but that it needs to be counterbalanced by exposure to, and experience in, nature. The more technology, the more nature needs to be in our lives.

Although he was initially talking about children, Louv's next book, *The Nature Principle*, shared how this view pertains to all of humanity.

Shortly after reading this book, I attended an educator's conference to see him speak. I found this message so important that I realized it was now part of my mission. But what would I do?

And it didn't surprise me when some of my interviewees were also inspired by Louv and the fact that his books confirmed their own purpose and mission in their lives.

I read an interview Louv did, following the book; he recounted speaking at a conference of builders and contractors to a mostly male audience. Louv shared a story of a place he visited as a child that was no longer there. Other participants also shared similar stories and the tone of the meeting shifted subtly into a more conscious, caring, earth-friendly dialogue.

If sharing these stories around a meeting room had this level of impact, what would happen if I wrote a book filled with experiences from famous people? How many people, who wouldn't ordinarily read about nature, would this book reach? Would reading this book expand their perceptions of nature and spirituality? Would it compel others to reflect on past experiences that they have dismissed or inspire them to "get out there" and have their own?

I held onto this book idea for ten years.

Write the Book

In September of 2020, while talking to a friend under a huge oak tree about what was next for me, I suddenly got a "divine download." The time was right. In the height of the Covid-19 pandemic, people had, more than ever before in modern times, been turning to nature for recreation and solace.

Cooped up in our homes for months at a time, with little else to do for entertainment, we spent our leisure time in the fresh air. Sales of outdoor equipment skyrocketed. National parks had their highest attendance rates ever reported. Even our local parks were filled with people exercising, playing team sports, or just strolling. And these trends seem to be holding up.

With the disruption of daily life, the entire Earth was on an historic pause. The pandemic allowed many of us to reflect and reconsider our lifestyles: where we lived, who we spent time with, and, mostly, our priorities. Many people moved, quit their jobs, or separated from their spouses.

This pause and redirection gave people time to reflect on their beliefs and purposes. In my own circles, I have seen many more people set on a path of spiritual awakening than prior to the pandemic.

Could it be the reboot, the time to reflect, or more time in nature? It's probably all of the above.

And there is an opportunity now to nurture the spark of a deeper spirituality, which has the power to transform us individually and globally. Now is the time when we must marry the rational and intuitive sides of ourselves, both our masculine and feminine. To continue our scientific quests while allowing the deep mysteries of the universe to inspire us with awe and wonder.

To date, there are thousands of studies demonstrating that time spent in nature contributes to greater physical well-being, reduces stress and depression, improves attention and focus, and contributes to a greater quality of life. But what about the impact of nature on our spirit?

That seems to be a bit jiggly.

While scientific research can objectively measure the positive impacts of nature on the physical body, we can only gather subjective reports of transcendence, awe, or other divine experiences of the sacred within the natural world.

> "By comprehending and strengthening the bonds between spirituality, science, and nature, we may come closer to achieving an environmental ethic that better equips us to confront two of the most imperiling crises of our time—global environmental destruction and an impoverished spirituality."
>
> —*The Good in Nature and Humanity: Connecting Science, Religion, and Spirituality with the Natural World*, edited by Stephen R. Kellert and Timothy J. Farnham

But we know that the way to wholeness must include a connection to nature. Not just from our minds, and through science, but with our hearts and through intuition. And there is a big difference there. Our minds want to understand how nature works and what benefits we can reap. Our hearts, on the other hand, want to build a relationship with the beings of nature. "What can I do for you?" is a question that most of us were not taught to even consider when communing with a tree.

And, as if I had asked this question myself ("What can I do for you?"), I was given a somewhat cryptic response one night, back in 2004. Out of the blue, I had a dream that I call my "Deer Dream" (which I share in greater detail in Chapter 10). I never forgot the dream, and in fact, recorded it in my journal because I knew it was an important clue to my life's purpose. But it is only years later that I realized that I indeed stepped up to the calling. I was told to help people understand the importance of nature in their lives.

Time in nature provides a powerful way for us to connect to the sacred. Even subtle experiences of the sacred in nature can shift us, and our lives, in profound ways. People who spend time in nature are more likely to live in a more compassionate, inclusive, earth-friendly way.

After the Download

When I decided to write this book—or, should I say, when Nature decided it was time for me to start—I turned to several helpful people for guidance, including my book coach, my astrologer, and a public relations professional in my inner circle.

I then emailed the agents of over a hundred celebrities, starting with those known for their environmental pursuits. Every few months I sent rounds of follow-up emails, as well as new ones to widen my range of people.

In November of 2021, when I reached the one-year anniversary of starting this process, while still receiving only rejections, I realized that I needed another path forward. I needed to start this book and see where it took me.

I decided to run a few practice interview sessions to see how my process worked. Did my preparation questions help the participants? How might the interviews unfold? Did I need an additional step that I hadn't considered before? And, most importantly, how much work would be required to write up their stories?

A few brave colleagues offered their help and so it began. Everything flowed fairly well, as planned, with a few minor tweaks.

But, unexpectedly, these stories really moved me. I felt like I was right there with them, experiencing through their words and emotions. I was so inspired that I knew, if granted permission, I would include them in my final work.

Then, I was struck with an idea. One morning, as I was going through my inbox, I received a weekly email from someone I followed who is a *New York Times* bestselling author. Spontaneously, I decided to contact her. I had admired her work about synchronicity and manifestation for several years. I loved her storytelling. And, a few hours later, I received my first "yes!"

Over the next few weeks, with the wind at my back and a newfound confidence swirling on my keyboard, I reached out to many authors and teachers, and others that I admired, all whose life's works were, in some way, connected to the natural world.

Within a few weeks, it was all coming together!

After a couple of months, I had an impressive list of participants and essays written.

In addition to my own experiences, I shared stories from people from a wide variety of backgrounds. Their stories of profound nature experiences have, for the most part, directed their lives and their callings.

I was on a roll. I got a literary agent through one of my participants. He was intrigued by the premise of this book and wanted to help bring it out to the world! Until, suddenly, the brakes screeched to a halt, and, for the next two years, there were no bites from publishers.

Nature teaches us the hard lessons of life. For me, I had to learn that this book would require the right timing. The stars needed to be aligned and, magically, that is what actually took place.

Two events occurred concurrently.

I was spending the day at Sweetbriar Nature Center, a local nature education center here on Long Island, with which I serve as a board member and volunteer, preparing for a big spring egg hunt, our biggest fundraiser of the year. We were decorating one of the hiking trails for the event called "The Enchanted Trail." We took a late lunch break, and I sat with a slice of pizza in the kitchen with the other volunteers and staff. I picked up my phone and scrolled through my inbox and saw the email. The email that made my year. It was from an editor at Mango Publishing, saying that they would, indeed, publish my manuscript!

Later on, I realized the synchronicity...the *Enchanted Trail*, and *The Enchanted Earth*. A spring egg hunt and the birth of my book. Spring has sprung! Such an amazing metaphor and symbolic beginning for this book.

Then, a few weeks passed, waiting for the contract. Just three hours after viewing the 2024 Total Solar Eclipse at the perfect remote cabin on the perfect remote pond in upstate New York, I scrolled through my inbox once we had cell service again. And there it was. An email, the contract attached!

Somehow, I intuited that, after this long journey of years, waiting for this magic moment, that it would happen the day of the eclipse. And here it was!

In many cultural traditions, a solar eclipse represents a turning point—a death and rebirth—the loss of light and the return of light. I had just witnessed this amazing natural event that only 2 percent of the world's population gets the opportunity to see. I was immersed in my own connection to nature, with an open heart and co-creative spirit.

The way the symbolism of these pivotal events mimics the focus of this book is undeniable!

What Surprised Me?

In my interviews with more than fifty people, as well as my private discussions with close friends and family, there were some surprising revelations about how we experience, internally process, and convey our nature experiences.

The first surprise was the realization that we often dismiss these stories. For many people, they forget or think their imagination ran wild. Consequently, there is no further exploration into these experiences. Their deeper messages, often carried through symbols and metaphors, are unexplored.

And that is such a shame!

In fact, as I was writing this book, I realized that some of *my* stories were unexplored as well. They were partly forgotten, until something in the writing process sparked my memory. I realized that the process of writing about my experiences opened up greater insight into the parallels, as well as patterns, that have appeared throughout my life.

I truly believe these experiences are like rare jewels, gifted from the sacred. They are to be savored, treasured, and reflected upon for the deeper meaning they hold in our lives. These stories are part of our personal mythology, enriching us with a deeper understanding of our true, authentic selves.

I am so grateful to have been guided to write this book through my encounters in dreams and in waking life. It has opened a door to the unconscious and subconscious within me.

One of the biggest surprises, even in the first few interviews, was realizing that I was the first person to hear their stories! This truly shocked me. While I was deeply grateful for the comfort and confidence they felt in sharing with me, I couldn't believe such heartwarming, inspiring stories had never been told to anyone before. Now, because of their participation, I'm so thankful that they finally have been.

And then there were a few that said that they had never shared their story because they questioned their mental stability. One even said that he asked a therapist if he might be schizophrenic. Another participant revealed an amazing story to me, and then, at the end of our session, he happened to mention *another* experience that was so emotionally moving to him that he cried for three days straight. But he would not share that one with me for fear of sounding mad.

I heard this from several people.

And some, even though they agreed to participate in an interview on a "profound nature experience" did not have one to share. What they eventually shared were not stories from the heart, but from the head—rational, logical accounts of a beautiful time in nature. (And I wonder, *Is there something deeper here to explore?*)

I thought to myself, *Don't we all have profound experiences that boggle the mind, which are difficult to even explain in words?* Don't we? Isn't the sacred or divine source speaking to all of us? And if not, why do some people have these experiences, and some do not?

I simply do not know.

After speaking to a few mentors, I concluded from these discussions that there is likely a combination of factors.

First, I truly don't believe that some people are "chosen" to have these experiences. I think we all have outstanding experiences that present opportunities to deepen our recognition of a sacred presence in nature. However, some chose to ignore these opportunities for a variety of reasons.

Some people may be in a defensive mode, closed off and unable or unwilling to experience life on a deep, emotional level. They might be facing difficult situations in their lives or shielding themselves, consciously or unconsciously, from past trauma.

Some people lack a worldview that embraces ambiguity or imagination. Without the conceptual framework to acknowledge or contemplate mystical experiences, they find it difficult to engage with such ideas.

When I was sharing the premise of my book with someone recently, he told me that he doesn't believe in "this stuff." Then he told me about an incredible story of synchronicity with his mother, who had passed, and his eyes got wide. "I don't know what to think about it," he said. I told him to just believe that it was a message from his mom. But he then squinted his eyes and shrugged his shoulders, as if to say, "Nah, it was all in my head." He just didn't have a worldview that could support an encounter like this.

I believe many people feel they misremember events and think their imaginations have run wild.

Of course, as mentioned before, some may think that their sanity is in question and never share the experience. History is full of stories of the insane who claimed to experience incredible encounters. And yet, religious scriptures tell stories of saints and prophets who openly claim to have experienced the incredible. But they were the "Chosen Ones" and that was "two millennia ago" when those things happened to special people.

What is normal? What is sane?

Is it sane to "soil our nest" to the point that we no longer have a home on this planet Earth? Is it sane to spend 90 percent of our days inside with little, if any, connection to the natural world that we evolved in, that has nurtured us for millions of years, and that offers the best release for stress in our modern world?

Jean Shinoda Bolen, Jungian psychiatrist, activist, and author, wrote about her understanding of openness to nature encounters in *Like a Tree: How Trees, Women, and Tree People Can Save the Planet*:

> Tree [nature] people are open to mystery...this openness creates the conversational field in which sacred experiences, synchronicities, and awesome dreams can be shared. These can be life-changing or course-changing when attended to, but no matter how powerful, they can be forgotten by people who become caught up in ordinary life. However, when recalled, even decades later, these recollections may be like seeds discovered in ancient tombs that could still germinate and grow.

> People are often cut off from their own numinous sources of meaning by others who have influence over them. Parents, spouses, peer groups, psychiatrists, and priests who have dismissed them, at best, or condemned them as sick or evil, at worst, made these significant experiences go underground. However, whatever was cut off or dismembered from consciousness, and consigned to the unconscious, still lives and can be re-membered.

The final surprise that I heard from nearly all the participants in this book was that they were so grateful to share their stories. They were grateful that I asked them to participate, and they looked forward to it getting out there into the hands of readers. And I am full of gratitude to them for sharing.

Hearing Our Shared Stories

I'm convinced that these stories are meant to be shared. Now more than ever, we, collectively, need to remember them, hear them, feel them. The more chaotic the outside world appears, we can, and need to, discover peace inside. That is how we need to *be* in this world, as we shift into higher consciousness in our human evolution.

The stories I've included are to spark your curiosity and remembrance of your own experiences. And, hopefully, to inspire the enthusiasm to create new ones.

When we reflect on our stories and are moved by the stories of others, we are more coherent and loving, and we send these positive energetic fields to others. We help raise each other up.

"The rising tide lifts all boats," is a quote famously attributed to John F. Kennedy. And yes, that is how we all "win."

Research shows that we can feel empathy for another when hearing their story. We vicariously feel what others experience.

I have thought about this for a long time.

So much of what we consume, as a society, contributes to fear and anxiety.

So let us soak in the yumminess of these sacred, profound stories of an enchanted Earth. Of beauty and love, of oneness and awe. Let's stoke the fires of wonder and play. And listen in. Pull our logs closer to the fire. And share our stories of profoundly positive, life-altering oneness with others.

CHAPTER 1

The Urgent Call

―

"The mountains are calling, and I must go."

—John Muir

―

Lead with Love

While working on this book in early February 2022, I was walking my shiba inu, Sadie, along the harbor front. The road meets the harbor at a tidal marsh, which extends across to the other side during high tide, connected by a culvert running beneath the road.

I've been walking along this road at least once a week for years, enjoying the sight of the shore birds, including the egrets, blue herons, red wing blackbirds, northern mockingbirds, and sparrows that bounce along the branches of black walnut, oak, and tulip trees, their songs ringing out through the marsh.

Sometimes I spot a herd of deer in a field, with one lookout monitoring my progress along the road. Less frequently, I see a family of raccoons climbing down from their perches in the trees at dusk to forage for food.

The land is abundant and alive.

On this occasion, the wind was gusting at twenty miles per hour and creating commotion in the canopy. As I walked along the inner marsh, I heard a moan. Then another. Then another. I stopped and said to Sadie, "What is that?" The moaning stopped.

At first, I thought that it was perhaps the sound of two branches rubbing against each other in the wind. But when the moans stopped while the wind continued, I knew that it must be coming from an animal.

I scanned the woods along the marsh in the direction of the moans, expecting to find an injured animal. But I didn't see any, so I continued on my walk.

When we returned, as I headed back toward my car, I heard another moan and stopped, silently searching. I finally spotted a small black animal moving its head back and forth. After a minute, I realized that it was a baby seal!

Seals are found in the waters around Long Island in the winter months, but seeing one is a rare event, even on the beaches. This one was far from the water during a very low tide, meaning that it must have found its way through the culvert during an earlier high tide.

He was trapped in a tangle of bramble, small trees, and dried grasses. He was struggling and I didn't know whether he was injured, but it was clear that he was exhausted and stressed.

Within a few hours, this baby was at a marine rehabilitation center, receiving hydration and medical care. And I was so grateful that I had chosen to go to the marsh that day and that I had the presence of mind to recognize an animal in distress.

I was told that he was about four weeks old, recently weaned from his mother. If he hadn't been found by the following day, he may have succumbed to dehydration, exhaustion, or predators.

As always, I tried to consider the message attached to such an unusual encounter in nature. In this case, what was the message that I needed to hear?

That area along the coast has played an important role in my spiritual discovery and growth for the last fifteen years. I have learned to hear the spirit of nature there. I have learned to share my own struggles and ask for guidance. The spirit of nature always responds and refreshes me.

That seal delivered an urgent message through the lens of metaphor: a call to action from the Earth Goddess (or Mother Nature, Gaia, whichever of the many names she is called). We need to take action. One act of kindness and compassion can be all that it takes to heal. A single, simple act that attracts many other simple acts, which lead to an abundance of positive, life-affirming action.

On a personal level, babies (both human and non-human) often represent the birthing of a creative project. Since the seal was four weeks old, he was born around the winter holidays, which was a significant time for me that year. That was around the time when I made the most progress on this book. I completed the bulk of interviews with the participants, and all my work for the previous year was finally paying off. This book was finally being realized.

I felt that the nature spirits were conspiring and guiding me to success. As my focus shifted to connecting with people that were likewise inspired and drawn to the natural world, everything unfolded like a purple crocus in the winter snow.

My dream was finally taking shape.

And the synchronicity of finding this lone baby seal, lost in the woods, was a metaphor for my foundering, trying to find my people: those who would not only be willing, but eager to share their experiences with the world.

And if I hadn't found him, that was also a metaphor. A metaphor for the urgency of this message for the planet. His cries were an urgent call to act.

It reminds me of something that one of my mentors told me years ago:

"The Earth is shutting down."

Those bleak words grabbed my attention. What did he mean, "shutting down?"

The words were stark, head-turning, but, after all these years, I... know...better.

The fear that those words evoke gets us nowhere. Haven't we learned, after decades of apocalyptic headlines? What we focus on grows. Let's try a different way of relating to this amazing world. A path of love.

The Great Shift

In the 1960s, social psychologist Erich Fromm coined the term "biophilia" to describe our passionate love of life and gravitation to things that are vibrantly alive.

Furthering this idea, biologist E.O. Wilson put forth his biophilic hypothesis that humans are genetically predisposed to be attracted to nature.

In the 1980s, the Japanese government conducted numerous studies that led to the practice of *shinrin-yoku*, also known as forest bathing therapy, to help alleviate stress and depression. In essence, to bring us greater well-being and sense of belonging.

From an indigenous, shamanic, and spiritually awakened perspective, we are in a momentous period.

This is a time of a profound shift in consciousness, often referred to as "The Great Turning," a term coined by ecologist and activist Joanna Macy. It's a turning point that we've all come here to witness and participate in. The Great Turning is a natural, awakened progression of our evolutionary process, from an Industrial Growth Society to a life-sustaining civilization.

But I strongly believe that we cannot get there through fear. The energetic frequency of fear weakens our immune systems and our ability to respond in a life-affirming way. It is only with the vibrations of love and curiosity that we can manifest this shift. Through organizations such as the HeartMath Institute and the Institute of Noetic Sciences, whose science-based research focuses on topics of consciousness and interconnectivity, the frequency of love promotes coherence. An energetic coherence of the body, mind, and spirit is required for positive action.

It is a state that I, and many in this book, welcome.

Why not lead with love? Cultivate a deep sense of kinship with the other-than-human world. Remember our unity? Recall that the Earth, and her spirit, is grander than the sum of her parts and more powerful than we can imagine?

Why not lean into the powerful experiences of her embrace that inspire awe and joy in our hearts?

As my friend Gordon Hempton said to me recently: We are not in an environmental crisis, we are in a spiritual crisis. Once we recognize that, then we can take the necessary steps toward self-love and love for this planet.

And this is what I hope the stories in this book will communicate: that we do not protect what we do not love.

A Poetic Language

> "Tao is a composite of everything, the intrinsic order of all things. The way we interact with Tao, with nature, is described by Yin-Yang...a tide of wind and water, a vortex revolving awhile rhythmically contracting and expanding (Yin-Yang) as we are carried along by the currents of Tao."
>
> —*Between Heaven and Earth: A Guide to Chinese Medicine*, Korngold and Beinfeld

Twenty years ago, during a time of great shift within me, I discovered feng shui, the Chinese art of placement.

I was forty years old and found myself in a career that no longer satisfied me. My home life was a mess as well. There were major behavioral challenges with both of my children, and my husband and I were just barely coasting through it, blaming each other. Everything that I felt sure about was upended. Cue a mid-life crisis.

During training, I would drive along the curving roads of Long Island's Gold Coast estates, lined with majestic trees. Specimen trees at the arboretum were labeled. I took walks during lunch, learning the names of these living beings, admiring their commanding presence.

Sitting in class for one weekend a month, I found all the topics that I loved in one place. Geology, astrology, divination, meditation, mapping and geography, floor plans and arrangements—and, most importantly, the overarching theme of the human-nature relationship.

For thousands of years, feng shui knowledge was passed from master to student through oral tradition. The literal translation of "feng shui" means "wind and water," the two primary agents of transformation on the earth. As such, feng shui is fundamentally centered on our relationship with nature.

Taoists understand that maintaining a healthy, abundant life requires us to live in harmony with the natural world. They understand that the masculine and feminine principles (known as yang and yin) are opposing but *complementary* forces of nature.

One of the ancient tools, called the Early Heaven Bagua, depicts the underlying structure of the universe. These natural energies are equally powerful forces, maintaining a sense of balance in their opposition: the universal opposites of heaven and earth, the elemental forces of mountain and lake, the impulsive forces of thunder and wind, and the organic forces of fire and water.

Taoists observe a life-force energy they call "chi," which animates all that is alive and connects everything to each other. When chi flows through topography, it animates everything in the landscape.

Through observation, Taoists learned about the cycles of nature: the circadian rhythms which track the sun's path through the sky, the monthly moon phases and daily tides, and the seasons. They recognized how these cycles are symbolic of the cycles of human events: birth and death, war and peace, and everything in between.

Eventually, a new system was developed to address this process of change in the Universe. This was named the Later Heaven Bagua. The peak of yin (receptive) energy—such as a seed germinating in the ground—is the Winter Solstice. Moving clockwise, the sprouting or birth of the seed is the Spring Equinox.

From there, the sprout grows to fullness, which is the peak of yang energy, or the Summer Solstice. This is followed by harvest and preparation for the coming yin, which is the Autumn Equinox.

Completing the cycle is the process of growing yin energy, which is the start of death and decay, in late autumn, and is followed by the Winter Solstice as the cycle repeats.

Taoist cosmology is very similar to the Big Bang Theory. It's a simple progression from Wu-Chi (at once, nothingness and the source of all things) to the spontaneous sprouting of "Ten Thousand Myriad Things" or all that is.

My exposure to this ancient poetic language of the land prepared me for a deeper discovery of my place in this world, and my purpose.

Spirit of Place

"I am a part of everything I see."

—Black Elk

Over the years, I have participated in retreats and workshops led by shamanic practitioners, and I am sympathetic to indigenous cultures and practices. In my limited experience with indigenous spirituality, I sense that they possess an understanding of right relationship with the land, with reverence, reciprocity, and kinship. They recognize the immanence of humanity within the universe.

After reading a few chapters of this book, one of the participants made a comment that gave me pause. She asked, "Where are the voices of the indigenous people?" True, the real roots and foundation of feng shui comes from an indigenous perspective in Asia. But what about the rest of the world, especially from Native Americans and First Nations people?

I reflected on that a bit. As a third-generation European American, having spent my life on Long Island, New York, I have had little exposure to indigenous cultures. My experience has been mainly through movies, books, and, as I mentioned, some shamanic teachings here and there. I have participated in sweat lodges hosted by Native-sanctioned practitioners, Celtic paganism celebrations honoring the seasons, and rituals led by Tibetan Bon monks. Yet I am removed from direct knowledge and wisdom of native people.

I cannot explain why I hadn't reached out to any indigenous people for this book. (I will rectify this in my podcast of the same name.) My selection process was intuitive. If I came across someone that sparked my interest, I reached out. It was not a conscious choice of omission.

Throughout my spiritual journey, I continue to develop this right relationship not only with the earth, but with myself. I have tremendous gratitude for the indigenous people and compassion for the hardships they have endured—the loss of their sacred lands, their wise elders, and, in many ways, their culture. I acknowledge that their perspectives, their values, and their ways of life are needed now more than ever.

I have integrated my studies with my experiences and have developed practices that resonate with me. I help people honor the land with the understanding that it ultimately helps them access an inner awareness.

This, I believe, is an indigenous way of living in this modern world of suburban tracts of land, often paved over with manicured gardens and the ever-present green lawn.

To help people witness the spirit of place. To be still. To observe. To pray to the spirits of nature. To the spirit of place. To hear the whispers in the wind. To acknowledge the unseen, the fabric of our reality. To know that we are just a thread woven into that web.

And I am grateful for those that allow access to these ancient ways of being that are about love, belonging, and connection. A way that allows the hearing and heeding of the feminine voice. I am a part of everything I see.

> "We often forget that *we are nature*. Nature is not something separate from us. So when we say that we have lost our connection to nature, we've lost our connection to ourselves."
>
> —Andy Goldsworthy, nature sculptor

To access this wisdom, you might expect that the stories of enchanted, mystical connections to nature would happen in faraway, exotic places. But you might be surprised to learn, as I was, that many took place in familiar locations: places where they had travelled many times or lived for years.

I realized that the locale is not important. What is important is how we show up to a place. To arrive with an open mind and an open heart: to be present, discover, and explore.

In fact, connecting with our land in an intimate way is a vital part of healthy living according to many indigenous cultures. We must acknowledge and care for the land, as she cares for us.

One day, while painting the window in my living room, I had a revelation.

I was up close with the white trim and experienced the subtle curves, corners, and crevices. My face was inches from the wall. I could see and feel all of its imperfections under my brush. I spotted a string of cobwebs I hadn't noticed before. The process created an intimacy with the woodwork that I had not experienced before.

A few months ago, I watched a documentary about Andy Goldsworthy, British sculptor and land artist, known for his ephemeral works using outdoor materials. In the movie, he said essentially the same thing. After spending months, over the course of many years, working with a tree that had fallen, he had become aware of its presence and every minute detail of its bark and branches. He had developed a profound relationship with that tree.

This experience is likely unfamiliar to many people who haven't developed a deep connection with their own home—those who don't paint their own walls or perhaps don't even decorate their rooms.

And this disconnection extends, perhaps even more so, to our exterior environments.

In my neighborhood, the landscapers pull up in their trucks and maintain several houses in a row, except for ours and a few others who do their own lawncare.

It was not long ago that most homeowners tended to their land. When I was a kid in the 1970s, nearly everyone mowed their own lawns. But now, for most people, that intimate connection has been lost.

One day, while at a client's home, I asked her where she felt special energy in her yard. A place she felt drawn to, where we could honor the land in our blessing ceremony. She looked at me quizzically for a few moments. Her property was perfectly manicured with a wooden deck, basketball half-court, in-ground pool, pool house, and "outdoor" living room gazebo. A chain link fence bordered the thick green lawn.

She finally pointed to her deck. She explained that she loved to sit there and look to the side of the yard, beyond her fence to the wooded area. It was filled with immature trees—having been recently converted from a farm with plowed fields—and a wild tangle of scrub brush. She explained that she often spied deer with their babies, lots of squirrels and chipmunks, and, of course, birds. None of these animals seemed to thrive in her yard. But beyond...that is where they lived. The wild beyond the fence. And this is where her unfocused attention flowed.

What part of her craved those wild, untamed spaces? What great discovery might she make if she allowed herself to go to that wild, untamed space within?

I see this often. We crave the wild. But we seek permission to go there.

All of nature has a story, wherever we go. Some of the stories involve geology and geography. Some of the stories follow the march of human history over millennia. And some of the stories are intimate and private. The land has accumulated all the energy, or chi, of what has transpired over time.

Some of that history is part of the cycles of nature, neither good nor bad. Volcanoes spilled their lava, creating new land. Glaciers scraped over continents, flattening the landscape before depositing themselves in the earth. Tectonic plates collided, creating new mountain ranges. Inland seas dried up, making way for salt deposits and leaving fertile soil for farming. An organic, ever-changing landscape.

But it's human history that creates change, for good or ill.

Building villages where our tribes could thrive, recognizing sacred places where people once worshipped or found healing. Yet much of history was filled with destruction—battles, death, grief, and sorrow. Mountains leveled for mining, fertile land stripped by short-sighted farming, and ancient trees felled for toilet paper.

I've worked with clients that live on land that contains the grief and sorrow of thousands of indigenous people who traversed the Trail of Tears. And communities built upon the only remaining farmland in the area, farms which devoured the rich soil with unsustainable farming practices and decimated wildlife with pesticides. Even on land near mining operations that use dynamite on a regular basis. Our land is scarred and hurting, even if the signs of it are no longer as visible.

Feng shui and geomancy has helped me to work with my clients to acknowledge the wounds and suffering with prayers of honor and reciprocity, connect with the beings of nature, and discover the wild places that long to be engaged with us.

Feeling the Life Force

Fifteen years ago, I started working with healing earth energy through the practice of dowsing. Dowsing is an ancient technique of identifying the invisible energy fields of the planet and cosmos using a physical tool; forked tree branches, L-rods, and pendulums are some of the tools that are commonly used.

Using these tools, dowsers can detect what the eyes cannot. They can uncover lines of energy in the earth, such as global grid lines, underground streams, geologic fault lines, caverns, and other areas of energy. From our perspective, positive energy contributes to health and healing. Negative energy, conversely, contributes to illness. And the major cause of negative energy in the earth is the behavior of humans on the land; areas of conflict, battles, major excavations, mining, and industrialization are all contributing factors.

I was initially skeptical of dowsing until I realized its power. After several years of practice, I started teaching an online course.

I would bring in guest speakers to broaden perspectives and techniques, and one of my guests was Dr. Jim Conroy, who has a PhD in plant pathology. He spent decades prior in the agricultural chemical industry, when, one day, he had an epiphany which radically changed his path from the very scientific work of pesticide management to intuitive communication and healing with plants and trees.

Jim, who became known as the Tree Whisperer, developed an alternative method of healing trees that was completely alien to his rigorous professional background. Few understood his new calling.

I met Jim and his partner, Basia, some years prior. In 2021, when Jim and Basia were sharing some new material with my students, *I* had an epiphany that would forever change the way I worked with dowsing.

For years, I had cleared the negative energy from my client's land. And I suddenly realized that was not truly helping them. But perhaps if I invited them into the process, it would complete the circle of restoration.

I started to ask them questions about the prior use of their land or neighborhood. If they didn't know, I asked them to do some research—historical, geological, cultural, and anything else that may impact the energy on the surrounding land.

I saw that discussing the previous challenges and tragedies incited awareness and, for some, a newfound empathy and compassion for the beings of the land, including the landforms, trees, rocks, soil, and natural bodies of water. I found that my clients were suddenly more engaged with the corners of their yards that were depleted or trees that needed some care.

In preparation for their honoring ceremonies, I ask clients to gather offerings during a mindful walk in nature. I ask them to share their intentions with the nature beings and see what presents itself for the offering, such as a feather or stone or water from a natural source.

I ask them where they feel drawn to do the offering, either in a spot where they feel the land is especially brilliant, or, conversely, needs some assistance. People intuitively know where to place the offerings. The land is speaking to them, even if they don't realize it. We then assemble by that special place, and I lead them in a simple ceremony of gratitude.

Years ago, I read a book about the daily spiritual practices of Bali, where they sprinkle flower petals along the threshold, doorways, walkways, and at their shrines. This beautiful, dedicated gesture to honor the Earth has stayed with me ever since. And I follow this practice every day with gifts of seeds, honey, flowers, compost, or even wine, all spread with reverence and conscious intention.

In her book *Like a Tree*, Jean Shinoda Bolen wrote that trees crave our attention. That message brings a big smile to my face as I imagine a little child, jumping up and down, saying "Look at me!" Yet it's also sad. How many people just walk by, oblivious?

With this shift in how I work, I am no longer "fixing" the "bad" energy in my client's land but expanding their awareness of and communion with the nature beings and spirits around them. And I invite them to cultivate this relationship with ongoing attention, gratitude, and care.

Too often we approach nature with the mindset of, "What can nature do for me?" Even though we may get out into nature and think we are in a right relationship, we may be engaging in a one-sided conversation. Perhaps we are looking to beautify the land for our own benefit. Or maybe we hope to relax and de-stress. But this is not a "right" relationship.

What kind of relationship can we have if all we do is take without giving anything of ourselves in return?

A healthy relationship requires reciprocity and asking, "What can I do for you?"

Message from an Oak

On a walk in the woods one afternoon, while writing this book, I did just that.

I encountered a large tree on the outer perimeter of the reserve. A nature educator friend of mine explained that the largest trees tend to be on boundary lines between properties. Those spaces where there is no incentive to clear the land.

I approached it gently and asked permission to connect. Once I felt welcomed, I laid my hands on her trunk. I silently asked, "Is there anything I can do for you?" I was present and listened.

After a few short minutes, I said thanks to the tree and turned to walk away. I had been hoping for inspiration as I was planning to write this chapter when I returned home that afternoon. I had hoped she wanted to share something.

And just as I started walking away, I was hit by a tremendous wave of sadness. I felt tears in my eyes. I knew these were not my emotions. They were coming from the tree.

She did not want me to leave.

But I swiftly recognized that it was not a message between her and I. She was addressing humanity on behalf of all nature.

It was then that a thought entered my mind: *The Earth wants us, but she doesn't need us. She doesn't need us for her survival.*

First, let's explore the fact that she wants us around. Are you surprised?

I think many of us are of the belief that the Earth is putting up with us, like we crashed on our cousin's couch out of desperation for a place to live. That she would be very happy indeed if we finally moved out and got our own apartment.

But no. I think nothing could be further from the truth.

The Earth wants us to continue living with her. We are her companions. The Earth finds joy in her connection and relationship with every one of us. Yes, that is the key word: *relationship*.

We are sentient beings and have a unique relationship with these strong nature spirits, unlike any other consciousness on this planet.

In the past, people were a delight for her. There was a sense of respect and honor toward trees, in addition to mountains, wildlife, the wind and water, all of life. Indigenous people co-created with her. She gave of herself freely to help humans, providing essential shelter and nourishment, weather patterns and seasons, and, more important yet, a psychological and spiritual connection to the Divine Source.

But there are so many of us who have lost this connection. Our perception is clouded by the physicality of life, by the delusion of duality, by separation from nature. And why not? Our contemporary culture suggests separation not only from nature but from each other, reinforcing competition and cultivating the ego.

Humanity is fueled by the economic realities of survival, with an insatiable thirst for the acquisition of material goods.

Our Westernized culture has indoctrinated us into valuing only this physicality of experience and what our five senses observe. We've starved our spiritual experience—our experience of the soul and unseen world.

For many people, the mere suggestion that there could be a relationship with a tree is ridiculous. To them, communication with nature beings sounds fantastical and relegated to children's stories and mythology.

Just the thought of hugging a tree makes most people laugh. Many tree-huggers, myself included, have been hesitant to hug a tree while others are around, for fear of being judged and ridiculed.

I hugged the large trunk of this oak tree. No one was around.

And then I received its final message, which was possibly more important and indeed ironic: the Earth does indeed *need* us. Not for sheer companionship, though, but to live to her fullest potential. To fulfill her fullest creative expression of being.

And then, as I turned back on the trail to continue on my walk, deeply grateful for her words and contemplating this crazy flip-flop in successive messages, things started to come into focus for me that I never truly understood before.

This new bit of information from the oak was fascinating!

Our attention, our deep respect, the honor we bestow in our relationship all allow Nature to be nurtured and more fully able to be Her best "self."

I related this new information to my background in Eastern philosophy. We are active participants in this "Cosmic Trinity," made up by Heaven, humanity, and Earth. The harmonic resonance of the relationship between humanity and nature, both above and below, is vital to the life impulse, the exchange of energy and consciousness.

We are the bridge between Heaven and Earth. Our full conscious presence allows for a divine balance in the Cosmos. We are positioned between the two realms as a mediator and distributor of chi.

Elizabeth Gilbert's book, *Big Magic*, inspired me to think even more about this idea of Earth *wanting* humanity.

Liz writes about creative inspiration as if it's a being, a consciousness, that is searching for a willing host to manifest ideas and creativity. This inspiration flows in the Collective Unconscious, from one person to another, until the idea is harnessed and brought to life.

This consciousness is searching for the right participant. Humanity, at least for now, is the only earthbound creature capable of manifesting her divine creative impulse.

We possess a unique consciousness. In the article "Touching Earth" by Steven Foster and Meredith Little, founders of the School of Lost Borders, they write: "Mother nature needs the ceremonies of humans if she is to reveal her sacred face to us."

We were a great team, the Earth and us! And we can be again. That is, when we quell our ego and listen to the messages in the wind and birdsong. When we walk on soil and feel the beat of the Earth. When we swim with the dolphins and hear the calls of the whales. When we ignite our wonder and curiosity and playfulness. When we are open hearted again. When we offer our respect, gratitude, and appreciation for our one and only home.

According to ancient philosophy, we are the mediators, bridging inspiration and manifestation. It all makes sense to me now.

Why I Am Hopeful

Considering all that is happening on our world, I am hopeful. I always was and will continue to be hopeful about our ability to do the right thing, eventually.

There is a lot of evidence against a positive outcome. But over the years—possibly as an attempt to bolster my viewpoint—I have sought knowledge to support my position. And I am happy to share a bit of my optimism with all of you.

When I was twelve, I saw the 1973 movie *Soylent Green* with Charlton Heston, heralded as one of the first mainstream movies to address climate change. Although quite traumatized, I was deeply stirred by the plight of our planet at the hands of the unawakened masses. I remember feverishly committing to myself that *this* was not the planet of *my future*.

It's interesting how I can now see the arc of my life that led me to this point, and this book. I don't believe that I said those words out loud to anyone. But it doesn't matter. It was a commitment, a promise, to the Earth and to my soul.

As a preteen, I somehow knew that if I gave into the emotion of fear about my future, I would contribute to the manifestation of it. It was then that I decided to create a future that was both bright and beautiful for all beings.

Another positive realization about our modern times is the realization that many of us are on a spiritual path. There has been an explosion of interest and access to various spiritual practices and teachings, including those from indigenous cultures around the world: Eastern philosophy, yoga and meditation, astrology and divination, depth psychology, ecopsychology, and mindfulness practices, to name a few. There are so many ways to access our inner lives.

With the sheer volume of us, we can and need to have our feet in both worlds: the physical and the spiritual. The seen and unseen. More than ever before, we can sense the magic and mystery of the Universe while walking along a garden path to our car or by watching the setting sun. We no longer need to retreat to a cave in the Himalayas, or a virgin forest, for spiritual awakening to occur.

Yes, as a species, we tend to be spiritually lazy. We are also skeptical. But spiritual realizations occur for many of us, spontaneously, with no preparation at all, during moments of openness.

Additionally, our experience of time has accelerated. It's not just our perception of time moving at a faster speed. Studies in physics show that both our universe is expanding and that the earth is rotating at ever-accelerating rates; therefore, so has our sense of time itself.

Why is this good news? I believe that our ability to learn is also sped up as well. We can learn and adapt so much more quickly than ever before.

Historically, apprentices would learn from their master for decades before they embarked on solo work. But now, we do not have the luxury of time. Knowledge, and integration of that knowledge into wisdom, can be obtained more quickly, as many of us are not learning but remembering these spiritual truths. C.G. Jung called this store of knowledge "the Collective Unconscious." We don't need to learn—we just need to remember.

According to Dr. David Hawkins in his book *Power Vs. Force: The Hidden Determinants of Human Behavior*, the higher our consciousness, the greater our influence on others. The more we work on the inside, the greater our impact on the outside.

As humanity ascends in consciousness, each incremental level is logarithmically more powerful and influential to the whole. A small percentage of the population can have a positive impact on the whole.

> "Look at the world around you. It may seem like an immovable, implacable place. It is not. With the slightest push—in just the right place—it can be tipped."
>
> —Malcolm Gladwell, *The Tipping Point: How Little Things Can Make a Big Difference*

And although in one reality it may appear that we are on the wrong track, the path is much more malleable than we realize. A slight push, as Gladwell says, is all that is required to shift everything.

Our kinship with all of nature runs deep. We just need to get out of our own way. As Salman Rushdie said: "The only people who see the whole picture are the ones that step outside the frame."

Let's step outside the frame.

While writing this chapter, I got the call late one evening that my baby seal was ready to be released into the ocean. It was scheduled for six o'clock the following night. Thankfully, I was free and rode an hour out to the Hamptons for his release.

I have seen bird releases before, and even did a few of my own (for a woodpecker, a possum, and a screech owl), but this was my first seal release.

It was an early May evening, and the wind was blowing. Me and fifty others gathered on the beach to see "Sweetbriar" shuffle out of his crate and make his way to the incoming tide. The wind brought up big waves, and he struggled to reach beyond them. His head bobbed up on occasion and then dipped below the waves. I felt a nervous excitement, and a pang of sadness. He was on his way, on his own. His survival would be up to him now.

And I couldn't help seeing the metaphor of the seal's release to the impending "release" of my son, Bobby, who was getting married the following month. After twenty-eight years, my son would also be on his own, out from under our care.

I watched Sweetbriar for a long time, even as most people left the beach and the parking lot. The shadow of darkness growing on the sand.

Seeing him out to sea was a fitting reminder of hope and optimism, and a poignant end to this chapter.

Invitation: Giving Attention

It really is this simple. Go out into a park or in your yard with an open, observant frame of mind. Give your attention to the trees, the flowers, shrubs, rocks, water.

That old saying, "Stop and smell the roses." Yes, do that.

Be present and observe the scene with all of your senses and with an open heart.

Perhaps ask the Earth, or a small flower, "What can I do for you?"

Then, be still and listen. Oftentimes, in my experience, sincere gratitude and the acknowledgement of their presence are all that is required.

Maybe you'll suddenly feel playful or happy. Perhaps you will be a bit sad. Allow yourself to feel. Let it arise and disperse.

CHAPTER 2

How Nature Speaks to Us

"Geologists have a saying—rocks remember."

—Neil Armstrong

Ancestral DNA

I got up and, suddenly, tears were streaming down my face.

The emotion just washed over me with no warning.

Now that I think about it, that feeling was the same one that I experienced the night when we first returned from our trip in Costa Rica. I woke up in the darkness and listened for the familiar call of howler monkeys, for the family of macaws...until I remembered that I was back in New York.

I broke down crying. It was so spontaneous. My heart ached. I felt a deep longing to be back in the embrace of the rainforest.

But this place, where my tears flowed so unexpectedly, couldn't be farther from the tropics of Central America.

I was in a wholly different landscape, one of my ancestors. A stark and muddy earth on the Isle of Skye.

There were no trees, just yellow grass which had not yet awakened to the cycles of spring. It was St. Patrick's Day. Streaks of snow still lingered from a rare storm the day before, resting in the ravines, dotting across the mountain slopes.

Why would this place evoke such emotion?

The tears just flowed, like the waterfalls behind me, as I looked out at the expanse of land before me. The mountains, created by eons of violent geology. Dormant volcanoes, eroded to the inner core, exposed, and manipulated by the onslaught of glaciers. This is what remains.

As irony would have it, I didn't plan on being here today. Didn't even have it on our itinerary.

As we drove from the mainland over the bridge to Skye, I kept our options open, unsure of what the roads would be like, or the weather. We had had our fill of narrow roads shared with tractor trailers and speed demons. Only the day before, we had gotten a flat tire in the amazingly beautiful Glencoe Valley. (FYI: Not a bad place to sit for a few hours while waiting for a tow truck on the side of the road.)

Today, however, our destination was an inn in Portree, the largest town on the island with a population of 2,300.

I suggested possibilities of what we could do (or not do) in the latter part of the day. To my surprise, my husband chose a hike to the Fairy Pools, an additional hour away.

The off-road to get to the Fairy Pools is part of the initiation preparation, as we soon found out. The road is a white-knuckled single track with pull-offs every hundred feet or so to allow passing. Often, the road would curve around a hill, requiring us to navigate, sight unseen, around the bend.

When we finally arrived at the car park, a jolly local fellow greeted us with a smile and a promise that our ordeal wasn't in vain. Was he a trickster gnome or an impish elf? It was St. Patrick's Day, after all. Still, I could have leaped out and hugged the man.

At first, the view of the trail was a bit intimidating. The path meandered, mostly following the riverbed, and wound its way as far as my eyes could see. Coming from the Northeastern US, I am used to forested trails that are hidden from view. This one, laid out completely before us, seemed long and intimidating, but it turned out to be an optical illusion. The hike was only three miles there and back.

Upon crossing the road, the gravel path dipped rather steeply, then leveled out, only to climb again up into the mountains.

When the gravel ended, a rough path continued. Winding over boulders, rocks, and mud, we hiked past all of the hikers we could see. We went beyond.

We looked for a place to put our feet in the water and climbed down to the river, perching on a few small boulders to take off our boots and socks, and roll up our pants.

For the first few seconds, I thought, *Oh, okay, not bad.* Perhaps that was because our feet became instantly numb! Not a minute later, we both exclaimed at the frigid temperatures. Indeed, it was still officially winter!

Months before, when Joe told me that he planned on putting his feet in a stream or loch, I thought to myself, *No way.* But here we were.

It was after this—after I had steadied myself on the rocks, dried my freezing feet with my socks, secured my boots, and stood up to face the view before me—that the tears burst out.

These magnificent mountains, called the Black Cuillin Hills, form a semicircle, embracing the entire site. My trained eyes recognized that it had perfect feng shui formation, often called the "armchair configuration" because of its comfort and support.

And I was standing in what's called the "dragon's lair," a sweet spot where the mountains gathered, concentrated, and focused their energy. Three of the Four Celestial Animals (the White Tiger, Black Tortoise, and Green Dragon) were evident in the mountains and hills before me. The final Celestial Animal, the Red Phoenix, a smaller land formation to my back, served to complete the bowl-like sensation of being contained. And I was standing in the middle of the bowl, delicately and softly held.

It's only upon reflection that I now recognize the importance of the water.

The energy of my ancestors lives in this water. Their blood, like water, flows in her veins, carried throughout the land.

The river enveloped me, merging me with the lifeblood of the landscape. She and I became one. Water is the conduit of all energy—electricity and magnetism. Water is life and consciousness, holding the essence of our DNA, capable of sharing and intertwining with all who resonate with her.

Although, at the time, I didn't see how the waterfalls or the Fairy Pools called to me, I see how she opened my third eye vision, to see beyond the physical realm to the majesty of the encompassing landscape.

This must be what a homecoming feels like.

The land of my ancestors, their energy concentrated and pulsing, seeing me, acknowledging me. Their memories were buried in the landscape, waiting to be awakened within me. All these years of waiting.

This was my homecoming.

At least three generations of my family have been disconnected from the land. My parents, grandparents, possibly even my great-grandparents did not know this land, this energy, this feeling. As with all immigrants, they left their homeland in search of a better life. But in that search, they lost something vital to their spirit. They left their hearts here, in this landscape.

I don't say these words lightly. I do realize that many grieved for their land long after they were gone. But the harsh realities of survival left them no choice. And for others, they were forcefully ripped from their land by oppressors.

Over generations, the separation and disconnection from our ancestral lands resulted in a hardening of our hearts, unable to be nurtured and healed by her energy. Unable to communicate with her, many no longer hear the messages of the robins and the glens. No longer feel the kinship with the oak trees and streams. The once open communication has been severed.

Was that why my elders didn't talk about where we came from? Is this why they didn't hear the stories of this land from their parents and grandparents? Were they unable to tell these stories because of their profound grief and loss? Was the trauma of resurrecting their stories too much?

We, in the twenty-first century, are the result. The earth, in her chaotic state, is the result.

As a child, I remember asking about our heritage, and all I got was, "We're here now and that's all that matters." My inquiries were shut down. I was told that it's all in the past. What was being hidden? What was too painful to recall? What had been lost? What stories of love and heartfelt connection were not shared?

I had no hint of that grief until now. The trauma of leaving, after many generations, was still embedded in this land. And the energy of that trauma burst open my heart.

Is the Earth Really Conscious?

Although I have had a deep love of symbols and metaphors my entire life, I never much considered the significance of where I lived. Only recently, I heard of terrapsychology, an emerging branch of ecopsychology which is concerned with both the physicality and energy of the places we inhabit, believing them to have streams of consciousness and meanings of their own.

According to a professor of ecopsychology, Craig Chalquist, terrapsychology is "a field of study and practice for understanding how deeply geographical locations (places) and geologies, trees, rivers, rocks, climate, weather, and other aspects of the world get into the human psyche."

In essence, terrapsychology explores how aspects of the places we have lived are deeply embedded within us and contribute to the development of our soul. They speak to us and remind us of who we are through imagery. Our conversations are both in waking and dreaming life. They inform and contribute to our personal mythology.

Consider this: If we identify with the land where we live, if it's crucial to our sense of self, then how deep would this connection be if we lived in the same landscape over the course of generations?

Many of us do not live in the land of our ancestors. We may live across the planet. We may live in a different country. Some of us have suffered this painful separation from the land against our will. Generations later, the lasting grief continues to resonate deeply within our communities.

Without this innate generational connection, mooring us to a particular landscape, climate, and habitat, many of us lack a feeling of relationship with the Earth. As a consequence, we struggle to comprehend our immanence within it all.

And I believe this is one contributing factor to our current ecological situation. The global environmental crisis we see in the outer world is a direct reflection of the spiritual crisis in our collective inner worlds.

The teachings of feng shui have helped me to understand that our balance has been upset. We are in a rare point in human history where we have the intellect and the intuition to awaken this dormant connection to nature within each of us.

This homecoming, the magic I experienced here in this place, restored and reconnected my soul. This is why I came on this pilgrimage to Scotland.

And it almost didn't happen.

Had Joe said, "Let's just get to the inn." Or had we stopped at the end of the paved trail. Or had we not paused in this quiet, empty space to place our feet into these sacred waters. None of this may have happened.

In a way, I've been planning this trip to Scotland my entire life. When I was little, my father joined the Scottish Clans of Long Island. He went to monthly meetings, and our family attended the annual Highland Games, a large festival with bagpipes, dancing, and unique Scottish sporting events such as caber tossing (or so I'm told).

My father was so proud of the plaque he received from the clan containing our motto, "Fac et spera" (meaning "Do and Hope") and the clan crest which is a hand holding a scimitar. Our family name, Matheson means "Clan of the Bear."

After my father passed when I was ten years old, I received a little book on Scottish clans from my best friend's mom. In it was a photo of our Matheson clan tartan and some scant information on the history and location of where they lived.

Those town names were emblazoned on my impressionable mind: Dornie, Plotkin, Balmacara, Kyle of Lochalsh. Faraway, magical lands, I thought.

But earlier that day we drove through some of these villages of my ancestors. We visited Eileen Donan Castle where two of my ancestors were constables, and one of them, John Dubh Matheson, died defending the castle in 1539. I saw the Matheson name on family trees, carved into castle doors, and engraved on war memorials.

These places we traveled through were fascinating; yet, there was something missing. They appealed to my mind, but there was no magic. No recognition within me. Nothing stirred my heart. I was in my head and tried my best to truly *feel* into these places. But nothing.

While planning this trip, I discovered the Viking roots of the Matheson clan, and learned that many of my ancestors also lived on the nearby Isle of Skye. This was new territory for me.

I was always attracted to Skye and knew I had to visit. Its remoteness stirred my imagination.

In an article by Alice O. Howell, Jungian analyst and Scottish emigrant to the US, she shared an experience in a waterfall on Skye. She talked about its spiritual healing power akin to the Japanese Shinto ritual called *misogi*. The waters offer a spiritual initiation for pilgrims. Years ago, I knew that I had to go there.

I didn't know what waterfall Ms. Howell visited, but it didn't matter. Any waterfall would be fine for me. However, since it was March, I knew that I wouldn't immerse myself completely, as she did. A quick dip of my feet would have to suffice. In retrospect, that was all I needed.

Spontaneous Embodied Connections

No matter how much we try to really feel a place, we cannot force connection. We cannot make magic happen. We cannot summon the unseen mystical beings that permeate the landscape.

It just happens.

It happens when we allow space. When we are still. When our hearts are open sufficiently to accept the spontaneous connection.

It's not likely to happen when we're among a crowd of strangers, marching through the landscape to get to a specific destination. People that say "wow," take a photo, and then walk back to their cars, another destination checked off their list.

No, these deep connections cannot happen when people brandish a selfie stick like a sword, wearing new shiny boots and white puffy jackets, looking perfect for their Instagram photo. It also cannot happen to an overwhelmed couple carrying a screaming toddler and pulling a stroller, just so they can check it off their list (no judgement—been there, done that).

I don't begrudge any of them for being here, for wanting to experience this amazing place. But if all they do is check it off their list, then they didn't experience a thing.

Not a thing.

Not a thing that this landscape wants to show. Wants to inform. Wants to awaken. Wants to enliven. Wants to inspire.

The stillness of the breath. The openness of the heart…an openness that is not truly possible with others around. Self-consciousness? Yes, a bit of that. Defensiveness? Perhaps that, too.

We just know when the feel is right…actually, it's the intelligence of our hearts that know.

When we are in crowds of people, with a few exceptions, we tend not to be fully open to experience. We unconsciously withdraw our energy to protect ourselves.

It's instinctual. Part of our evolution. It's the same defense mechanism that we use when we walk onto a crowded subway.

But when the energy field is synchronistic, when the vibrations are light and soft and subtle, out in nature, we tend to drop those natural defenses. The energy of our hearts can blossom. We vibrate at a higher frequency. We enter a state of higher consciousness.

This is the sacred. In the sacred places of nature.

This is where our ancestors, all our ancestors, prayed and worshipped the Divine Source of all things.

They were in tune with nature and felt oneness with it all.

In landscapes like this, the Divine Source is palpable. Nature spirits, angels, fairies, guardians of the land, genus loci. We can feel it. The Divine is immersed in the landscape. Its presence waiting to be picked up by our radars. *But it's so subtle and still, we can easily miss it.*

I could have missed it that day, as I stood up from the river to leave the Fairy Pools. My head was full of travel plans and next steps. But the river washed all that away. There was nothing left but the void. An opening within my core, between heaven and earth, that allowed direct relationship. And what occurred in this brief moment in between—in this rift in space—was true connection with the Source. A golden, shining thread connecting me to all that is.

But one of the craziest things about this experience is that...

I almost did not remember it!

Incredible. Inconceivable. Yet, it's true!

How could this amazing experience be quickly forgotten by me, who had been working for a few years already on this book of sacred connection?

I do not know what happened.

Was it the mundane task of returning to our travels? Navigating back along the treacherous path to the main road? Perhaps that is part of it.

But there must be more to it.

Then I realized that it takes a willingness to experience the grief.

It takes courage to feel this ancestral pain. The pain of my ancestors in leaving this land, even though it was almost certainly done for the promise of a better future. Pain from that void is still felt by subsequent generations who often have no understanding where this grief is from, or perhaps that it is even there. A gap we have attempted to fill with material excess, alcohol and drugs, or endless distractions.

The pain of losing our evolutionary connection to the land, to our relationships with its spirits, and to our direct connection with the Divine Source.

Upon returning, I had a conversation with Kathleen, a good friend who has a strong psychic ability and often taps into messages for me. Whatever she communicates to me rings true in my deepest core.

On this call, I wanted to share my excitement about the trip. But as usual, whenever I called her, I was also feeling ungrounded and frustrated with my current work projects. I needed to hear her words of inspiration.

Over the last few years, since the early part of the pandemic, I have been creating new online classes and writing nonstop. I've been in "doing" mode. But project after project failed or sputtered along. I could see that I was spinning my wheels, going nowhere.

Was it my timing? Was no one interested in what I was saying?

Or was it a sign of something bigger?

Three years later and I still felt like I was in this whirlwind. Things were changing. I was changing. All this time, Pluto, the planet of major spiritual transformation, has been at the cusp of the fourth house in my astrology chart—the place in the birth chart relating to the deep beliefs that form our foundation. Pluto was driving me to dig up old beliefs about myself, what my family taught me to be true, and, yes, ancestral connections.

At the same time, it was also deeply transforming my career. The two parts of me—my spiritual beliefs and my life path, my career—are one.

I was being asked to review, rethink, reimagine myself. I was being asked to release old patterns from my life and from my ancestors, perhaps from previous lives.

Pluto's impact has felt like a slow, deep rumble of thunder, subtly shaking my entire foundation. And one morning, as I was contemplating Pluto's position in my chart, that happened in the physical realm.

The highway department rolled in earth-moving equipment (I cannot make this up!) and decided to tear up the road to fix the potholes that existed only in front of *my house*! All the time, my entire house shook and rattled.

Such a striking metaphor. I pondered. What did I not want to see? Did I not realize that change was inevitable? Was it that I got too comfortable with the way things were, or how I was going about my work? What outdated beliefs did I need to release?

Kathleen patiently listened to my stories of Scotland and then to my angst, to the restlessness behind it all which was unnerving me.

And then she said, "Only when we are moved, can we be moved."

Her words sent tingles through my body.

Then she asked me to recall a place on my journey that had *moved me*. She said, while shaking her head knowingly, "You know what I'm talking about, Maureen. A place that felt like you were coming home."

My mind suddenly stirred into a blur, wondering what *place* she was talking about. There were lots of places we hiked and explored. So many beautiful landscapes. *A place that moved me...*

And it was only then that a brilliant white light seemed to shine from the top of my head. Or was it my mind, opening up to the possibilities that these words offered?

I recalled that moment of tears, and I suddenly *knew* the place. I knew it for the first time...its potent message of true connection.

Tears came to my eyes. I recognized the significance of that moment, that place, and the synchronicity connecting that moment to *this* moment. Spirit stirred me to remember.

For spirit had made it clear...remember.

Throughout our trip, I was mindful of being present in the moment, of being still and listening with all of my senses. I whispered silent requests for connection. I laid my hands on ancient stones and cairns and trees. But I felt nothing. Received nothing that I was aware of.

I realized that we cannot force a relationship. True connection is subtle, quiet, and soft. It happens when we least expect it.

We are not the telephone linemen installing the connections. We are the receivers, not the doers.

In fact, I realize that being in "do" mode prevents connection. Connection happens when we are open and patient. When we wait and watch for the spark of electricity, resonance, and symbols to flow. Or not.

Kathleen then said, "When you are moved, you can move others."

And then, I realized the importance of this book, which had been floundering for the past three years. I felt a renewed sense of obligation to get it published and into the hands of others. I realized that if I can assist in moving others in any way, that is my goal. And that is exactly what my purpose is.

Our Relationship with Nature Evolves

John is a friend of mine who has worked with trees his entire career. As an arborist, he is hired by mostly residential clients. When he was a young man, climbing to dizzying heights was an adrenaline rush. He felt a sense of freedom and skill at bringing these trees down. But as the years went by and John mellowed, his relationship with trees matured.

He slowed down and started noticing a presence in the trees. He felt their life force. Eventually, he noticed a consciousness, or what might be called a "wise soul."

"These trees have been here for maybe a hundred years," he said. "It pisses me off when a client complains that they make a mess in their yard. Even though it hurts my revenue, I do my best to convince them that the trees are worth so much more than they realize. They provide shade and reduce their cooling costs. Trees increase the value of a house. But even monetary rewards don't convince most of my clients to keep the trees."

After conversations with others like John, I began to wonder: *Do people inherently have a connection to trees and nature? Or is it learned?*

I am deeply curious.

As the nature vs. nurture debate continues to evolve, I think that yes, we do inherently have a deep bond with nature that can either be nurtured or severed by our experiences—and, perhaps most importantly, by our caregivers.

> "If a child is to keep alive his inborn sense of wonder, he needs the companionship of at least one adult who can share it, rediscovering with him the joy, excitement, and mystery of the world we live in."
>
> —Rachel Carson

For many people, that relationship with nature is dormant and may be deeply buried in our psyche.

What would it take to activate that connection?

> "We will never be truly healthy, satisfied, or fulfilled if we live apart and alienated from the environment from which we evolved."
>
> —Stephen R. Kellert,
> *Birthright: People and Nature in the Modern World*

Josh Heath is a forest therapy guide who takes people on mindful walks into nature to inspire connection. He says, "I have done over 350 forest bathing walks and most of my participants have deep experiences with nature, and some, for the first time."

And, as I have witnessed, some of the people who have the deepest experiences can be surprising—not what you'd expect.

A couple of years ago, I was co-leading a session with Josh. One of the participants was probably there because of his wife. He didn't seem to want to be there. Josh opened the session and guided us to our first "invitation" or encounter with nature. He suggested that we approach something that grabs our attention and just sit with it.

All the while, I could see out of the corner of my eye that this gentleman was texting and scrolling on his phone. We came back as a group to share, and he admitted that he was not fully engaged. So, we walked to our next invitation in the meadow.

This time, the man's cell phone was properly stored away in his pocket.

When we reached the meadow, we stood silently, as an immature red tail hawk swooped above our heads. After giving us all a show, the hawk finally settled on a tree branch not far from our group, as if to observe us.

When we did our share, the same man said that he was deeply moved by a message from that bird. Somehow, he perceived that the bird was telling him to slow down, to be present, and to witness the beauty around him. He was so full of gratitude.

As a feng shui consultant, I also experience this disconnection from nature and our environment. Many clients have said that they do not feel that their home is "home." They are energetically disconnected. I used to think it was about the structure itself, but now, more importantly, I realize that it's all about their disconnection with the land.

When working with my clients outside on their land, I often sense a new opening of their senses. As if they are truly seeing the land for the first time, be it their own yard or surrounding neighborhood. Their inner knowing, or third eye chakra, is suddenly activated, giving them a direct connection to their hearts. I have seen the surprise on their faces, as they soften and see the land for what feels like the first time.

One client in Connecticut had three large boulders on her property, called erratics, which were deposited by glaciers millions of years ago. They were front and center, right next to the driveway. When I mentioned how amazing they were, she replied, "What boulders?"

But once we walked over to them, she discovered a newfound sense of appreciation for them. I pointed out that one looked like the head of an eagle. Then she started seeing other animal shapes in them, too. It was quite magical!

The realization that her landscape was alive, even the rocks, was something new and curious to her. Geomancy, which interprets features of the landscape for guidance and messages, has been practiced in many cultures all over the world. Regrettably, geomancy and many other earth-based practices have been seen as the superstitions of primitive people.

But there has been a resurgence of the concepts of consciousness and aliveness in other-than-human beings.

I love that my work helps others to see this reality. That they can uncover a deep love for their land and nurture that relationship, for the benefit of themselves, their communities, and the Earth.

How Can We Inspire This Connection?

When visiting Honolulu for the first time, I got to Waikiki Beach and checked into my hotel, preparing for a week-long conference.

After bringing my bags up to my room I headed down to the beach. It was late afternoon, and the beach was filled with tourists. But that didn't keep me from having my own personal connection with Diamond Head.

As a child, I saw images of this dormant volcano every week on the popular TV show *Hawaii 5-0*. I had never thought much about it and didn't anticipate seeing it, but there I was, standing before it, and I was overcome with awe. The shadows and light of the setting sun stopped me in my tracks.

It was unexpected, which I think had a much greater impact on me. I compared this experience to my first trip to the Grand Canyon. I was expecting it to be awesome, but when I stood at the overlook, the experience was less than profound. It's hard to explain, but I think my anticipation dampened my reaction.

My time in Scotland confirmed to me that I cannot *expect* magic to happen when I visit a sacred site. I cannot *control* the experience. There are two consciousnesses. Us and the other—be it a volcano, a tree, or a vast landscape.

So, if we cannot command this deeper connection with nature, then what is the purpose of the experiential exercises in this book? I wondered about that for a bit. *How can I help others who want to have an experience, a story to share?*

It is true that we cannot expect a profound experience in nature. But there are things we can do to prepare ourselves, to be open and available.

I've realized that it's not unlike desiring anything that requires the participation of another person. We are not able to *acquire* a new friend, a romantic partner, or even a publishing deal. (I've learned this the hard way!)

But we can prepare ourselves in many ways that create space for things to happen.

The exercises in this book are invitations to experience. Ways to work on being present, mindful, and still. To approach nature with an open heart.

To spend time outside in communion with beings of the natural world. To learn to listen and observe with a soft gaze and open imagination. To ask for guidance and receive a response in some form.

Aren't there some basic ideas that help cultivate connection? Sure, there are.

Those super-magical, cloud-parting, bush-burning experiences are rare, but if we are each open to a relationship with nature, we can have many beautiful, heart-stilling experiences that will nurture our souls.

I bet that you already have plenty of experiences that can be recalled easily by you or may spontaneously arise as you read these chapters. Our memories may be a bit hazy at first, but, given some space, the stories will unfold.

I think we have all experienced things in nature that we cannot explain—at least with a rational mind. Oftentimes, these stories are explained away as ordinary life, until there is not a shred of magic left.

As you read the stories in this book, keep an open mind. Step into the realm of childlike wonder and curiosity. And perhaps you'll be able to maintain that frame of mind to reflect on your own stories.

But in order to reflect and uncover greater meaning in our experiences, we must orient ourselves to the languages of nature.

The Language of Metaphors & Symbols

How does nature speak to us? And how does she stir emotion and meaning?

Nature speaks to us in a symbolic language. We "hear" this language with our ears or eyes, even bodily sensations, but it's a much more subtle experience than we are used to noticing. I liken it to hearing a dog whistle. We need to shift our frequencies, like a radio dial, to hear the sound.

And sometimes, the message transmitted simply results in a gut-felt, deep knowing.

I believe it's different for everyone, and it can be different for each experience.

This mode of hearing is different from what our structured minds are accustomed to. We are taught that nature is a source of resources to be exploited. We've suppressed the natural activity of the right brain and heart center where these subtle connections are made. But the wisdom of traditional ways of thinking is rising and reactivating these long-dormant faculties.

When we were children, we hadn't learned the difference between reality and imagination. Our relationships with nature and her beings were open and unencumbered by modern norms. However, for many of us, our imagination was stifled in adulthood. Our "stories," which include the breadth of human experience that cannot be measured and proven, were no longer considered "real."

I discovered my interest in mythology only recently. Prior to this, mythology would exasperate me. Why would the characters' names change? Why would the stories morph with each telling? Why did the moral of the story vary with each telling?

These inconsistencies led me to cast mythology aside.

But alas! I realized that mythology resides in the realm of metaphor and the Divine Feminine. Myths are fluid and ever-changing; they cannot be boxed up. Mythology exists in the realm of the unseen. It's a shapeshifting creature that requires softness, open hands, and imagination. Our rational minds need to switch off.

Psychologist and mythologist Dr. Sharon Blackie says that mythology "helps us reclaim the lost voice of the Feminine." Myths are deeply rooted in place, in the land. And we have forgotten how to listen.

Dr. Blackie adds that we are in "mythic times." That we must dive deep to reclaim the lost voice of the Feminine, mythology, and the land. I believe that our stories will contribute to this recovery of the Feminine and the restoration of our connection to the natural world.

Through my discussions with many people over these past few years, I have discerned that communication with nature takes many forms. Some people hear words, but not with their ears. Sometimes they see something—though it's usually in their mind's eye. Some report images, a feeling in their bodies, or just a sudden sense of knowing.

Messages are often experienced as symbols to be deciphered, but sometimes they are communicated as plainly as can be.

But what is common among all of these people is that these experiences have deepened their feelings of connection with the universe and infused them with a sense of something larger at play in their everyday lives. These experiences are treasured, contemplated, and, sometimes, shared with others. But not often enough. I've heard equally from participants that this was the first time they've shared their story. There are various reasons for that.

It became clear to me after writing this book that these stories make us feel more alive, and even just hearing about them can have a powerful influence on how we feel about ourselves in the world.

In this next chapter, I share the stories surrounding what many people have experienced in nature. It's a great place to start since I believe you, too, can relate to them.

Invitation: Observation

If you are engaging with nature in a conscious way for the first time, the most important role you can play is that of an observer. This may sound easy, but it's harder than you think. When I sit outside or step out for a walk, I find myself recapping the events of the day or pondering an issue that I need to resolve. I occasionally open YouTube and listen to a favorite podcaster.

There is nothing wrong with any of these behaviors, but if you want to be open to nature communication, your psyche needs to be available.

I mentioned that sometimes I find myself pondering an issue I need to resolve. That can be helpful as an exercise.

Ponder the issue or decision that needs to be made, and then turn your attention to what is occurring around you. Observe the sky and landscape for more-than-human activity. A sudden breeze, a bird flying past, a sound.

Sit or walk for at least fifteen to twenty minutes. Take note of what you observe.

For example, while writing this chapter, a Cooper's hawk landed on a tree outside my office window. I got up to watch her. Then she swooped down, apparently in pursuit of lunch, under a shrub in my yard. She came up empty, looked around, and flew away. The next day, I noticed two clumps of white bird feathers along the curb outside my house. I assumed she found her meal.

What meaning could you ascribe to that experience? If this was you, how might you interpret that for a situation you are currently in?

CHAPTER 3

Heart-Opening Awe, Oneness & Grief

"There are two ways to live: you can live as if nothing is a miracle; you can live as if everything is a miracle. The most beautiful thing we can experience is the mysterious. It is the source of all true art and all science. He to whom this emotion is a stranger, who can no longer pause to wonder and stand rapt in awe, is as good as dead: his eyes are closed."

—Albert Einstein

When people first encounter mystical experiences in nature, it's typically when dealing with a sense of loss. These experiences help us feel oneness with the natural world. I believe that most of us have experienced this.

Awe is defined as reverential respect mixed with fear or wonder. It's often accompanied by a feeling of transcendence or of existing beyond the limits of our ordinary reality. A feeling of oneness or unity with all the universe.

Awe is evoked by a stimulus in our environment that dramatically expands the observer's usual frame of reference in some dimension or domain. Examples include places of great natural beauty, like the Grand Canyon and Niagara Falls; vast products of human ingenuity, like the Great Wall of China or the Eiffel Tower; and works of art that help one see the world through new eyes, like Van Gogh's *Starry Night* and Picasso's *Guernica*.

In studies of awe, findings show that awe is often accompanied by a feeling of transcendence—that which is beyond—of a spiritual or religious nature.

An experience of awe is usually spontaneous and unexpected.

Sue, an amateur nature photographer, was vacationing on the South Island of New Zealand. Urged by fellow travelers, she visited Milford Sound for a kayak tour.

Sue shares the scene, "That day, when I stepped out of our rental car for our early-morning arrival at the launch site, the scene of the fjords nearly overtook me. The majestic mountains rose up almost straight out of the steely gray water, while the sun was still over the other side of the mountains. At one point, one of our guides pointed up to a waterfall way up on one of the mountains. It seemed small and insignificant. Then he told us that the waterfall was taller than Niagara Falls! All sense of scale was blown away."

The scale and vastness of nature can take our breath away. We quickly realize how small we are in the vastness of the cosmos, of life. Awe has the ability to put us back into our place. To instill gratitude and a humble attitude for being a witness to the Divine in nature.

According to research, the experience of awe moves people from a "me" focus to a "we" focus. It can lead people to feeling kinder and more generous—qualities we could all use more of.[1]

---

[1] "The Science of Awe," September 2018, Greater Good Science Center, John Templeton Foundation.

Clinical psychologist David Elkins discusses transformative experiences of awe in his 2001 essay, "Reflections on Mystery and Awe."

He writes, "Awe is a lightning bolt that marks in memory those moments when doors of perception are cleansed and we see with startling clarity what is truly important in life. Moments of awe may be the most important, transformative experiences in life."[2]

Nearly half the stories shared in this book feature components of awe and transcendence. Some were sparked by fear, such as stories of wildlife encounters and raging storms, while some were inspired by a quieter reverence at the sight of a sunrise or a small rock on the beach.

Since I've been writing this book, the subject would come up often when in conversation with family, friends, and new people I met. As I recounted my work, eyes would widen, heads would shake—yes, they knew what I was talking about. And they often wanted to share their story with me!

By far, one of the most common stories of connection is the appearance of a bird representing a loved one who recently died. Perhaps you've experienced this, too.

Connecting to nature is as simple and profound as that. In those moments, we are open to connection and observant of our surroundings. Our hearts are more open than usual due to grief. And we make the leap between the bird and our loved one because we are looking for solace and peace.

This chapter shares stories of awe and oneness, as well as overcoming deep grief through the embrace of nature.

---

2   Elkins, D. N. (2001). "Reflection on Mystery and Awe." *The Psychotherapy Patient*, 11(3–4)

"I remember thinking, *these are the last moments you might have*. Nature has a way of giving you strength and perspective, which is hard to replicate in any manmade environment."

—John Kiesendahl

The Healing Waters

In 1958, when he was eleven years old, John "JK" Kiesendahl's parents bought an old boarding house in Pennsylvania. The ad in the *New York Times* was vague about its location and the contact phone number was in Brooklyn. JK's father called and spoke with the owner.

> When my father found out where it was, he was incredulous. He yelled up to my mother, "Hey Mary! The property is on Lake Teedyuskung!"
>
> When my parents were sixteen, my grandmother brought them both to stay at a girlfriend's house on a lake in Pennsylvania. It was Lake Teedyuskung. While there, my parents walked to the end of lake, and as the story goes, my dad put a stake in the ground and said something like, "Someday we will return."

A month after the exciting call, JK, his two other siblings, and his parents left their home in Huntington, Long Island, and moved to the woods. JK attended a one-room school with six other kids in his class. At the inn, his father was the cook and the business manager, and his mother, well, she was the heart of the resort.

The area was extremely undeveloped, unlike his suburban upbringing on Long Island. But in summer, it was like a different place when it was in full swing. Everyone in the family helped out, yet there was always time to hunt, fish, explore, and swim in the lake.

Some of JK's fondest memories include paddling a canoe all the way to the other side of the lake. That area had a small wetland separating it from another, smaller lake. They would portage over and have the lake completely to themselves.

There were snapping turtles, beavers, otters, and snakes. And nothing but trees all around. Hilda, the owner of that land, didn't mind them being there. On this old, worn-out dock, he and his siblings would sit, fish, and enjoy the quiet of nature.

In time, his parents' boarding house blossomed into a small resort. JK left to attend Cornell University for hospitality and then served as a naval officer for a few years.

After a childhood of working in every type of position, JK knew the business inside and out. Not long after he returned, at age thirty-four, he bought the resort from his parents. He took his passion, perseverance, charm, and warm heart and tripled the resort's size to become a year-round family resort.

> We were always expanding. We built a golf course a few miles away, which received environmental awards for its irrigation techniques. But we needed a backup plan for periods of drought. It was then that we purchased Hilda's property, which was just across the street, for the use of the lake water.

Suddenly, during the expansion of the resort, JK's oldest child, Robert (lovingly nicknamed Bob), was diagnosed with leukemia. JK shares, "Bobby was an athlete, so some of his symptoms were attributed to sports injuries. No one thought to check his blood. And he was diagnosed very late."

They went to specialists all over the East Coast, but no one gave him a chance of survival.

At the time of the diagnosis, Bob was only twenty-six years old and newly married. He and his wife were expecting their first child. It was at this lake, sitting on the old dock, where Bob found his sanctuary. This land hadn't been developed yet. It was still just a lake in the woods.

JK's son would sit there—sometimes alone, sometimes accompanied by loved ones—contemplating the acts of living and dying. The serenity of nature allowed Bobby to let his mind wander. He found peace, acceptance, and even gratitude while surrounded by the woods, bog, wildlife, and nature.

> I would sit on the dock with him and talk about life and what's next. We both found great strength there. It was a very emotional time in my life. And I know that being surrounded by the spirit of that land and the lake helped both of us brave the challenge of getting through this period within our family.
>
> It is amazing to think that this very same spot, where I found sanctuary as a child, would be so enormously important later in my life. The time we spent there was really special.
>
> Sitting with him was a bonding experience. I remember thinking, *These are the last moments you might have.* Nature has a way of giving you strength and perspective, and this is hard to replicate in any manmade environment.

As fate would have it, Robert was blessed to be accepted into an experimental bone marrow transplant in Seattle.

> The day before he left for Seattle, I thought, *This may be the last time I'll have with him.* I didn't know when—or if—he'd be back. I told him that I loved him. It was a very spiritual, tearful day. But what stood out the most that day was the feeling of true hope.
>
> We are truly blessed to say that Bobby did return, six months later, and eventually recovered from his illness.
>
> A few years later, a couple who had been long-term guests at the family resort suggested that we consider partnering to build a spa.
>
> I remember thinking that this was an interesting idea and walked them over to this property. It was a beautiful, sky-blue day in the spring, and when we reached the little lake, that very special place on the dock, two eagles flew over our heads. I saw it as a sign from heaven!

With that, the seed of an idea sprouted, and a partnership was formed to build a new spa resort. They made sure to build the spa facilities far from the lake in order to maintain the pristine nature surrounding it and the naturally occurring cranberry bog nearby. JK truly wanted to honor this sacred land.

The lake shore is a cranberry bog, made from glacial ice over ten thousand years ago. It is recognized by naturalists because of some of the endangered species of plants that grow within the bog.

Originally, the desire to preserve the area and natural habitat as much as possible was an emotional one. The team at The Lodge at Woodloch is so lucky they did, as they have learned much about one of their most precious resources over the years. Still, to this day, they are mindful to maintain the integrity of the land; to be in harmony with the spirit of the land.

JK adds, "Of course, I visit the spa often and try to make it a point to visit that dock (a newer, sturdier one), and every time I cannot help but recall that time with my son. I am so grateful for the peace of this land. It's a big part of our lives."

Twenty-five years later, Bobby, now part-owner of the family of resorts, manages their charitable work. In addition to donating to leukemia organizations like BK Hope Cures, they support a nonprofit, For Pete's Sake, based in Philadelphia, that provides families of cancer patients the opportunity to go on a retreat in this sanctuary in the woods.

> The healing power of nature has been a powerful force in our lives. We truly believe that this special place in the woods helps our guests to find connection, wellness, and healing in challenges that they may be facing—both big and small. We are humbled by the fact that we can be the backdrop on their journey—inspired by our surroundings like our family has been, time and time again.

Transcendence

Our magical connection with the land and sky is derived from tapping into this ancient tradition of coming home. When nature embraces us, especially in the vastness of a landscape, we feel awed. We suddenly remember how small we are in relation to the cosmos. And rather than feeling inconsequential, we realize how inconsequential our challenges are in the immensity of the universe.

When grieving or dealing with challenging situations in our lives, we often go out into nature. We instinctively know that the natural world will hold our grief without opinion or judgement. Mother Earth, the archetype that we ascribe to the consciousness of the Earth, is so named because of the feeling of care and compassion that we receive when we are in her embrace.

Nature reminds us of the seasons and cycles of life and death. When we are immersed in our plastic world, we often forget about the ebb and flow of our lives. Wherever we find ourselves today, however low, it will not last.

Change and transformation are the only "given" in life. We can witness the opening of a cocoon and see the new butterfly struggle, then spread its wings for the first time.

There is great comfort in realizing that tomorrow, the sun will rise again, as it did today. There is the freedom of space, space to process our thoughts and emotions. Again, awe and feelings of transcendence play a significant role.

In a 2008 study at John Hopkins University, researchers theorized that an experience of transcendence might help terminal cancer patients deal with the stress and grief accompanying their diagnoses, and perhaps allow them to feel greater peace when facing death.

Because awe-inspiring experiences in nature are harder to find in a lab environment, they used psilocybin, also known as magic mushrooms. As part of a controlled study, participants were brought into the lab and were interviewed before and after ingesting psilocybin. Findings showed that two-thirds of the participants rated this experience as one of the five most spiritually profound experiences in their lives.

Anecdotally, in an article about the study, "What a 'Transcendent Experience' Really Means," written by Emily Esfahani Smith, she discusses this experiment through the eyes of one of its participants, Janeen.

"There was not one atom of myself that did not merge with the divine," Janeen shared.

Why did this help?

David Yaden, psychologist at the University of Pennsylvania and lead author of the paper, suggests, "When the self temporarily disappears so too do many some of these fears and anxieties." Janeen's fear of death melted away, she says, because of this study.[3]

Nature helps us cope with illness and can help us process grief from the death of a loved one.

> "Winter always turns to spring."
>
> —Nichiren Daishonin, Buddhist priest (1222–1282)

Fire in the Sky

This is an appropriate quote to open this story shared by Sumita Singha. Today, as I was writing, we had an unseasonably mild day in early March. A promise of spring that will soon be here in earnest.

Yet, at the same time, we are also witnessing the devastation of global wars. We are observing a period of death and rebirth on a large scale, both physically and energetically. Many astrologers are saying that we are in the throes of one period ending and another beginning. A shift in archetypes, from the Age of Pisces, which represents tradition

---

3   www.thecut.com/article/what-a-transcendent-experience-really-means.html.

and the patriarchy, to the Age of Aquarius, representing revolution and the collective.

This theme, based on the cycles of nature, is not only helpful in understanding where we are, but in providing us hope for what is to come.

Sumita, a lifelong Buddhist and chartered architect, shared how being in nature has helped her deal with periods of grief or illness.

Being a Covid long-hauler with heart issues, Sumita has found relaxation by being in nature and sitting near trees throughout the pandemic.

> I almost felt like they were talking to me. At those times, I found that I couldn't talk to anyone. However, I felt not only free to share my grief but found solace and empathy arising out of those exchanges.
>
> One tree on my visiting routine was a 230-year-old plane tree in a park nearby which must have been planted during the Victorian times. I felt that I was in the presence of something quite ancient, yet young. Trees lose their leaves every year but every spring they burst back to life with vitality and health. Apparent death always results in a resurgence of youthfulness and vitality. There is great comfort in that.
>
> We don't give trees the respect that they deserve.

Sumita grew up in a busy commercial area of New Delhi, India. "We were poor. I lived with my parents and two sisters in one room with a leaking roof. At one point, I even slept on the table that was also used for my studies and eating." Her family were tenants of her aunt and uncle, who lived on the ground floor of the house. The uncle and aunt were childless and with their parents being busy, the girls spent a lot of time with the uncle.

But every summer they spent two months in her father's village in West Bengal, India—1,200 miles away. There were no roads, electricity, or running water.

> We had to entertain ourselves. We used to explore the river, the forest, and the canal, which had an old Banyan tree growing next to it. I became an expert at climbing trees. One day, I got stuck upside

down in a lime tree, with my leg held tightly between two crossing branches. Just so I didn't attract the attention of my father and get scolded, I had to hang there quietly for a couple of hours until my cousin passed by to hold open the branches and let me out.

My uncle grew roses and would take us every year to the Delhi Rose Show. What beautiful flowers! I learned how to draw and paint them, using very bright colours, because I saw how glorious nature is. I wasn't shy! Those experiences impacted the way I paint. What I learned was that flowers always do their best. And that was a big influence on how I live my life. Living my very best version of myself.

Every year as a child, Sumita witnessed the breaking of the monsoon season. She would climb up to a shared wall between her home and a neighbor's, where she could watch the clouds as they turned pink at sunset. "I would feel so serene, watching those clouds."

She says, "When I was six, I saw the full moon in the sky and started crying. My family didn't understand why I was crying. But it was the first time I understood human mortality, as if the full moon had told me something."

In 2012, when Sumita was living in London, her beloved uncle died at dawn in India. "He had a beautiful smile that always reminded me of the full moon smiling back at me. And that night he died, serendipitously there was a full moon. I thought of that time when I cried as a child. As I looked up at the moon from my window in London, I felt his warm, embracing presence."

A few years later, Sumita received a call from India that her father had died in New Delhi. He had been a brilliant math teacher but suffered a lot of discrimination in the big city as he had come from a humble village; later in his life, he developed acute schizophrenia and Parkinson's disease and became blind. For the last five years of his life, he had been bedbound. According to tradition, he was to be cremated within twenty-four hours. Unable to fly back to India in time for that ritual, she felt a deep sadness. Being the eldest child, she felt she had an obligation to be there, which weighed on her.

But standing at her window that evening, Sumita saw the most glorious sunset. "It was unusual for that time of year! The colours were deep reds and golds. A wash of peace fell around me. I felt that my father was saying goodbye and telling me not to be sad. It was as if I was witness to the cremation after all. It was alright. I would be with my family shortly for the service. I didn't feel bad after that."

In his novella, *The Bridge of San Luis Rey*, American writer Thornton Wilder wrote, "There is a land of the living and a land of the dead and the bridge is love, the only survival, the only meaning."

Sumita used her connections to the natural world to help her through a painful childhood, as well as through challenging times throughout her life, including the death of loved ones. And the experience of oneness and transcendence she received has further solidified her understanding that we are of nature. There is no division. Her father is the sun, and her uncle, the moon, forever smiling brightly in the sky.

If an amazing landscape can help us deal with the death of a loved one, but even a small mountain lake couldan help wash away the pain of trauma for a little girl.

> "I knew that the lake was alive and conscious,
> and aware of me."
>
> —Llyn Roberts

Immersed

Llyn Cedar Roberts has written about so many of her amazing experiences of and in nature in her many books. But she hasn't shared much about her special childhood place, until now.

> I grew up very close to Milton Three Ponds on the border of New Hampshire and Maine. As one of three bodies of water that stretches well over a thousand watery acres, as a child the Town House Pond was to me a beautiful, expansive lake.

This lake had been loved by her family for generations. Her father and grandfather swam here as boys, just as Llyn did as a child. Llyn's two children, now in their thirties, spent many of their early years living near the ponds and swimming in this lake as well.

When she was young her cousin had a cottage on the largest lake, Northeast Pond, so she spent many warm summer days either there or at the public access beach, swimming in that water body.

> I can recall being there so clearly. It was such a visceral experience from my childhood. The smell of the lake and the air became one. An earthy, organic scent—when I took it in, it pervaded my whole body and being. Scents can so powerfully evoke feelings.
>
> I remember the feeling on my skin and body as I was entering the water of this lake. Sometimes I would just dive in and take the cold plunge. Other times I'd slowly walk in, which was more challenging to do as it was sharply cold! It didn't matter if other people were around; I felt such solitude. It was as if I were alone there, just the lake and me.
>
> I felt such oneness, as if I truly belonged there, in the water. I remember spending a lot of time submerged under the water, with the muffled sounds bouncing in my ears. It was an escape from everyday life. Sometimes I was not even moving, just feeling the buoyancy, the temperature, just feeling immersed and embraced by this underwater world.
>
> Even at that young age, I was in touch with spirit of place. I knew that the lake was alive and conscious, and aware of me.

Llyn had a challenging childhood and being in that water, she felt cleansed and healed. It cleansed her entire body inside and out. She felt her troubles washed away, absorbed, and transmuted by the waters.

> We have our social reality. We live in a world of people. People are obviously important. At the same time, what the lake taught me is that we are also of the Earth and nature. It's just as important to relate with trees, water, air, sun, fire, and the stars. These are in fact our primal relationships that remind us of the essential aspects of who we are. Nature nourishes us in every way, including spiritually.

As so many of us do, Llyn found her refuge in nature. She found it incredibly healing and restorative, helping her to understand who she is and that her primary relationship must be with the Earth. The Earth is what sustains and nourishes us in the most basic physical way.

> I was in touch with the seasonal rhythms and personalities of the lake and what the qualities of the water and air were like at different times of day, including early morning and at sunset. As I used a rowboat and fished in different parts of the lake at times, I was familiar with many of the coves and bays.
>
> In the winter, there were ice fishing huts and winter festivities. When my children were young, our family would skate and walk across the lake when it was frozen. I recall hearing stories about my grandfather harvesting blocks of ice from the lake for ice boxes back in the early 1900s.

Some time ago, after many years of absence, Llyn returned to the lake and immersed herself in its waters. It was like no time had passed.

> Lakes have consciousness. We all can open to a sense of oneness with nature, as this is intrinsic to being human. It's also unique for each of us. For me, when I experienced that oneness, environmentalism comes naturally. Through our love for nature,

> we are healed and embraced by her; in turn, we gain a powerful sense of wanting to communicate with and care for our planet.

Many years after she left New Hampshire, Llyn added a second "L" to the name she had been known by for decades (Lyn). Llyn is the Welsh name for lake. Serendipitously, she was a Buddhist practitioner for many years in Boulder, Colorado in the 1980s and had received the Boddhisatva name, Fearless Dragon Lake.

> That lake is an essential part of my childhood, of me. It held me and gave me a sense of who I am. I now live three thousand miles away, but I travel to the lake in my imagination quite frequently. It's in my body; it's in my heart.

In Llyn's work of many decades, she leads transformational programs for people to experience this deep sense of oneness with nature and to know the natural world as conscious, alive, and aware.

"I was desperate to feel that sort of communion again and scared that the sensation couldn't be replicated. I'm glad I was wrong...but it took me a while to find other doorways in."

—Maia Toll

In the Flow

As a child, Maia was both terrified of, and madly in love with, horses. Her first word, according to family lore, was "horsey." So perhaps memories were shining through from a previous life.

Since the time she could sit on a horse, Maia was in lessons. For the first eight years, panic was a constant companion. Her progress was painfully slow, and she remained one of the lowest level riders, still mastering simple horsemanship skills. So, when her parents agreed to buy her a horse, they aimed to find one that was gentle and slow.

But one windy Saturday morning, Maia found the complete opposite. One that was high-strung and nervous. Her trainer told her not to bother getting on, but Maia had gotten used to moving through her own fear. She decided to approach the mare. Watching the horse roll her eyes as the wind whistled and branches creaked, Maia had an epiphany: the horse was more scared than she was.

After all the years of lessons, this quivering, shaking mare taught her something none of the well-trained lesson ponies could. Just like that, a switch was thrown in her mind. As Maia got a leg up into the saddle, she focused on the horse's fear instead her own...and that changed everything.

While that particular mare was not the horse Maia ultimately chose, her newfound empathy suddenly made her the rider who was assigned the least predictable animals. And her riding skills quickly progressed.

It was no surprise that when she finally found her horse, Indy, he was a bit of a wild card. She was thrown from the saddle often. Despite her efforts to calm Indy down, he remained wild.

Until one day, Maia had an experience that changed not only the way she rode, but the way she thought about spirituality. This transcendent moment became a cornerstone of her thinking of what it means to be human, and she has spent the years since trying to replicate it in a variety of ways.

It was a cold winter day when she was fifteen years old and took Indy to the indoor arena. Yet again, Indy was shaking his head and throwing his feet around, telltale signs that he would soon start bucking.

Her trainer came to the end of the ring and instructed Maia to do figure eights in a small circle. The figure eight exercise was a tactic used when either the horse or rider needed to focus. It helped to settle the horse into a routine and was a pattern which required the full concentration of both rider and horse.

> We were bending one way, then the other. As the rider, you are part of the bend. Holding your legs, carving the horse's body in a

> semi-circle. Each turn requires slight shifts with your legs and body. The horse connected to my movements and breath, in a state of constant focus.

Back and forth they rode. They became attuned to one another. Their breath in sync. A sense not of her individual body and the horse's, but of a shared body. A sense of being out of mind, as well as out of body.

The horse calmed down.

At this point, the trainer had them move into a trot. Round and round, over and over, for thirty to forty minutes. She lost track of time and slowly slipped into a liminal space—a space that many have described as "flow."

She didn't know how long this lasted. But it was long enough to know that she wanted to experience it again.

> When that experience happened on Indy, I had crossed over the threshold from novice to greater mastery. We cannot go from zero to sixty, and don't often take time to perfect the craft. But when we do, there is a point when our physical motion becomes more automatic.

For several years, she equated this experience with horseback riding, thinking that horses, in general, were the key. But eventually she realized that the key is repetition, like a chant. In this space, you're no longer thinking about what to do. You transcend the physical, the mundane, to the metaphysical plane. Allowing your consciousness to expand beyond the body.

> I call this magic. This is where magic resides. In communion with plants, trees, and wildlife, you can communicate and change things without your ego getting in the way.

What she experienced, so many years ago is the state that mystics aim to achieve. And over the years, Maia has discovered visualization techniques that can get her into this space very quickly.

> When in this state, you are watching your own body in awareness of others as if was part of the self. But it is not an ungrounded

experience. You're aware of the world around you, but it's no longer in duality. No longer in an egoic state of mind. After experiencing this state, people can get stuck there. But it's so important to learn to toggle back and forth between transcendence and everyday reality. To know both states.

"I learned to listen to my heart with courage."

—Vanessa Champion

The Utter Silence

For Vanessa Champion being on a mountaintop is sanctuary. In her travels around the world as a photojournalist and documentary-maker, she has often found herself gravitating toward mountains in her journeys.

She shared a story about a holiday in the Jura region of France, near the Switzerland border. She stayed in an old gîte-style chalet with two levels up on a mountainside, overlooking a little remote village.

One late afternoon, while huddling up hygge-style with cushions, candles, and fondue on the balcony featuring a 280-degree view, the sky began to darken, and a dramatic thunderstorm began to saturate the wide horizon with a midnight blue billowing of clouds. The sky became overcast, and the lights in the village below came on, responding to the darkness overcoming the valley. There were huge dark clouds advancing over the nearby mountain ridge.

> As I looked at the wide horizon, I saw the fingers of lightning coming from the clouds, reaching down to touch the Earth below. One after the other, like spiky specters of vitality from above, igniting the Earth with energy. I remember thinking it was the awesome power of Gaia, doing her thing. The rain bearer.

> Although we were high up, I still felt safe and protected. I felt a sense of freedom within me. Connecting to the inner free spirit, and the fire within myself.

As she recounted these stories to me, she described more of what the mountains taught her.

> I recall the morning after, such a contrast, hearing the alpine cow bells from the slopes close to the gîte, the soft breeze stirring the edelweiss, and the lush greenery of the mountainside. I saw the little cheese van driving through the village below, and thinking life goes on after a storm, balance is restored. There is light and life after the darkness. I thought, *I want to live here, in France, in these mountains, where I can witness the simplicity of life every day.* I'm still yearning for it.

Something else about the mountains that struck her was the quality of light.

> It's different up there. I guess my passion in photography is to capture these special but simple moments. And capturing the ephemeral light is magic! I love to share the beauty with these virtual windows into nature.

She talked about the expansive views at the top of the mountain and how it helped her reconnect with a challenging time in her youth.

> I went through a period of trauma when I was seventeen years old. Within the span of a year, I lost thirteen people—family and some friends. I was quite a rebellious teen, but still had great grades in school. I was Cambridge University bound until that year threw me off-balance. It seemed relentless. So much death in such a short time.

What that period of her life gave her was a call to live every moment.

I decided to live my life to the fullest. To appreciate what was around me, every day. Even if it was just birdsong at my doorstep.

Vanessa went on to establish a nonprofit called the Global Photo Aid Foundation, that connects charities with photographers and filmmakers to help raise awareness of their causes, including human and animal rights, and the environment.

On one such trip to Nepal, to support a promotion of the Mahasiddha Sanctuary for Universal Peace, she visited the Shyalpa Monastery in Kathmandu. She shadowed Shyalpa Tenzin Rinpoche, who was entrusted with this parcel of land, next to the birthplace of the Buddha, in Lumbini, Nepal to build this sanctuary.

At this time in her life, she was undergoing another transition. She was pitching to be the editorial director for a London newspaper with circulation of over 50,000 subscribers.

She shared her thoughts at the time:

> I was battling imposter syndrome. Can I do this? Should I do this? Am I good enough? I knew taking this project on would be another change in my life. I was worried it would take me out of my comfort zone, though I had run publications before. I took the opportunity to discuss my concerns with Rinpoche, who discussed with me the Tibetan Buddhist teaching called "The Path of the Warrior."

She also had some amazing dreams inspired by the landscape near the monastery in Kathmandu, which Rinpoche interpreted.

> I realized that we are meant to rise above the challenges we face in our lives. I learned to listen to my heart with courage. It was a really interesting experience to be immersed in that sacred place. I came back from this trip with a *"Let's go for it!"* mindset.

While staying in the monastery which sat high up and on top of a hill overlooking Kathmandu, she had time on her own to wander around outside the monastery. One afternoon, she walked out of the monastery gates and took a trail around the side of Kopan Hill, where she saw sweeping, beautiful, awe-inspiring views below.

> The silence and harmony of the green farming land steeped onto the hillside below on the edge of the city looked almost fuzzy in the early-morning mist, like an impressionist's painting. And the orange earth beneath my feet, kicking up little dust storms behind me, reminded me of the orange robes of the monks, like the spiritual intent was even under my feet. The energy was hard to put into words, but like sunshine, I was soaking it all up. Breathing in through my eyes.

She still recalled, "I sat there, above the clouds, and was overcome with a sense of harmony. There was a beautiful feeling of peace. The wide vista struck me as awesome."

Music has always played a big part in Vanessa's life. Being a musician and documentary filmmaker makes her keenly aware of the importance of sound. "Sound is as important as what you see."

> There on the mountain was utter silence. I've sought out mountainous landscapes throughout my life. Up there is silence. The silence of the clouds as they move through the azure sky, the mountains standing strong, eternal, in a still hush. At one with myself, nature, the moment, life, earth, sky, divine presence. I want to—crave to—commune with that.

Prayer flags were fluttering with the winds. She said the air was so pure and that the simplicity of it all was breathtaking. Vanessa said she felt clarity. She explained that her life has always sbeen full of work, to-do lists, commitments. Doing a thousand things, meeting a thousand people; going here and there.

> But the air in the mountains gives me time to think, to process, to breathe. The air is pure, crystal clear, fresh, new, untainted, transparent, fresh, and expansive.

It's interesting when I reflect now on these experiences. Each time, my life was in a period of change. I felt a shift coming in my life, whether it was a relationship, or career, or other personal transition. But these encounters with mountains helped ground me and seemed to bring me back to myself.

Dealing with Life's Challenges

Witnessing the bigger picture, of which we are a small part, is a common experience in nature. This mystical experience brings us into a state of awe and understanding.

Back to the article on transcendent experiences, Yaden writes, "Most people have had some sort of transcendent experience at some point in their lives—and about one third of the population has had 'intense experiences of unity.' "[4]

It doesn't have to be as dramatic as life and death.

Experiences in nature can help us process the grief and stress of other major life transitions.

A few decades ago, I was going through a time of great stress. My son was being unofficially diagnosed with ADHD because of his behavior in school. There were phone calls and trips to the principal's office. There were conversations with family and friends. At the time, my husband and I were on different ends of the spectrum. I was leaning toward getting an official diagnosis and perhaps putting him on Ritalin.

I see now how this episode was a pivotal time for my personal growth. I was so anxious over my son's behavior and how it reflected on me. At the time, I defined being a good mother as having well-behaved children. And the current situation made me feel like a failure and unable to control how others judged me.

My husband was furious with me.

[4] www.thecut.com/article/what-a-transcendent-experience-really-means.html.

One evening at dinner, the topic came up and we got into a screaming match. I jumped up from the table and went outside and started walking. I needed to move and get into my body in a physical way. But I did it instinctively, not purposely.

I live across from a high school, so I entered the school field where I walked off my grief and anger.

My heart was pounding, as tears streamed down my face. It was an awful, gut-wrenching time. And although I wish I could say that I had a profound realization of peace then, I can say that my walk under the expansive sky as it was darkening for the night helped me regain some sense of stability and calm. It would be a long journey ahead, but the stars and moon embraced me that night, heard me, and gave me solace. Over the coming years, being in nature helped me move through this situation and many others that would come after, with greater calm and grace.

Invitation: Processing Grief

We all carry grief at different points in our lives. Many times, grief for something past is still present deep down.

Go out to an expansive landscape, such as a beach or mountain view. Perhaps go to view the sunrise or sunset when fewer people are around, if you feel safe. Just allow yourself to feel your pain. Imagine the pain being dark smoke that you discharge with each exhalation, and breathe in golden light from the land and the sun.

Spend at least twenty to thirty minutes being present, in quiet observation. Perhaps bring a journal with you to write down your thoughts and what messages you receive from the natural world.

Alternatively, you might want to immerse yourself in a body of natural water. Imagine the water nourishing and cleansing you of all impurities and imperfections. There is a reason why nearly all the world's religions utilize water in rituals. Feel the healing surrounding and nurturing you.

CHAPTER 4:

Invitations to Connect with Trees

"All the trees around my yila were glowing like fires or breathing lights. I felt weightless and at the center of the universe..." And when he looked back up..."[there] appeared a woman dressed in black... She was green...from the inside out...this green was the expression of immeasurable love."

—Malidoma Patrice Somé, *Of Water and the Spirit*

There is something about an old, gnarled, majestic tree that captures our imagination. The dark forests of fairy tales seem to connect us to an ancestral mythological remembrance. We feel their presence within the landscape. Trees evoke a sense of mystery, reminding us of our place within their vastness.

When we see a grand tree, we pause and take it in with all of our senses. We notice its sturdy trunk. We observe the graceful arc of its branches. And its shape against the backdrop of the sky. There is something so deeply pleasing about a beautiful tree.

Throughout human history, trees have been critical to our survival, in physical and metaphysical ways. They have been a place to worship, to live, and to thrive. Trees nourish us with their shade, shelter, and production of oxygen.

But trees are so much more than that. They are pure magic, mystical beings that hold secrets beyond our understanding.

When interviewing people for this book, so many of their stories involved trees. Just as I shared my experience with that magnificent oak tree that "told" me that it was time to write this book, many of us have had messages relayed to us, whether we realized it or not.

Trees possess powerful energy fields that can "cleanse" our stressed and chaotic energy with their gentle, luminous presence. This is the essence of the practice known as forest bathing.

Some of us are more sensitive to their energy than others. We can feel the pain of trees being cut down in our neighborhoods. We feel great distress, as if we lost a loved one.

The larger a tree is, the greater its positive influence on the environment. And that is why the disappearance of nearly 90 percent of old growth forests in the US (75 percent worldwide) is so concerning.

Trees are enchanted and alive with consciousness. And we can rekindle this awareness by spending time with them.

> "It's not the treehouse, dummy, it's the trees. It's nature. What I love doing—creating and building these treehouses—isn't important. It's about the experiences that people are having in nature because of the treehouses."
>
> —Pete Nelson

The Best Darn Cocktail Party

Before he was the Treehouse Master, Pete was building single-family homes in the Seattle area and dreaming of a career building treehouses for adults.

Although he had received a bachelor's degree in economics, he had a gift for building.

He built many forts and treehouses in his childhood backyard in New Jersey. "I always loved architecture. I drew houses as a kid. I would plan out my treehouses on paper first. My paternal grandfather had a tool shop, and we would build model sailboats and sail them on the river. I realized that I was a decent builder. What I could see, my vision, in my head, I was able to create."

About two years after college, Pete turned his attention to building homes. But he wanted to be "the treehouse guy."

> I was visiting with a friend of mine who showed me this cute little treehouse he had built in his yard. It was the quintessential kids' treehouse. Even then, I thought it would be cool to build these for adults. Having ADD, I really appreciate smaller projects. To create something on this scale is more palatable. It gives me a great deal of satisfaction.

He said he was so excited that he went to the bookstore (there was no internet then) and found only a couple of books on the subject.

> Over the next few years, I built treehouses wherever I could, took photos, and eventually published a coffee table book of my work in 1994.

That was the beginning of his business.

In the mid-90s, there was a lot of press about a major run on redwood trees in Humboldt County, California. The trees were on the last 3 percent of privately held redwood forest. Roughly three thousand acres of trees were being decimated by the Pacific Lumber Company for profit.

Julia Butterfly Hill was the most famous protestor that camped out in these trees. Hill spent more than two years sitting in what she called Luna, a two-hundred-foot majestic tree, until an agreement could be made.

> It was 1996 and I was captivated by how this could happen. I decided to check out these trees to see how I could possibly help. I found a guide that took me into Headwaters Forest. We snuck onto the land, behind the gates.

The guide took Pete to the battle zone: the boundary line between the standing and the fallen trees. One side was bright sunshine, the other darkness from the abundance of foliage.

> There was an enormous amount of tension. All at once, a deep feeling of tension and sadness overwhelmed me. It was palpable. I couldn't believe my eyes. How could anyone want to devastate this land for money?

Coming from the East Coast, the size of these redwood trees captured his imagination. He had driven on redwood highways and through the parks. But those experiences could not compare to what he was experiencing now.

> Understanding that these could all be gone in a very short period; trees that lived for eighteen hundred years, just gone. I suddenly realized that this deep emotion was not just from me, but from the trees themselves. The energy that the trees were giving off was like a fearful human. He said he realized that the trees were fearful of our presence.

Their energy felt withdrawn, as if they were on the defense.

> "Who are you?" they seemed to ask. "Are you coming to take us out? Are you sizing us up for the chainsaws?"
>
> It was like they were holding their breath. The emotion felt very real. I just cried. There are no words.

Then Pete noticed a giant salamander on the forest floor, right by his feet.

> It was probably five inches long with a long, big belly. It was early in the day, still cool, so he wasn't scurrying off quickly like they typically do. But I just looked at him and felt his presence. He was like Yoda. He turned his head and looked up at me, and I thought, *What a wise, gentle creature.* He seemed to say hello. He was friendly and welcoming.

He said that's when his frame of mind changed.

> The trees seemed to sense that they we safe. From then on, it was like a cocktail party with the most interesting, wise beings. Giants! They were full of wonderous energy. They were delighted to have me there. I was thirty-four years old at the time, and I felt so clearly like I was having the most extraordinary experience!

And it was then that Pete suddenly had an epiphany among those redwoods. "It's not the treehouse, dummy, it's the trees. It's nature. What I love doing—creating and building these treehouses—isn't important. It's about the experiences that people are having in nature because of the treehouses."

He was able to redefine his life purpose.

> It's the power of nature that reduces us to the feeling that we are a small part of the whole, a deeper connection to everything—realizing that was a beautiful experience. The redwoods wanted me to see how joyful and happy they were in their environment.

He said he was in the presence of 1,800-year-old beings, still in the prime of their lives.

> Trees don't move anywhere. They stay in one place and deal with whatever weather throws at them, be it high winds, freezing temperatures, mudslides, even fires. But they get everything they need, as well. They survive and thrive in the most amazingly magnificent way.

This experience filled him with a renewed sense of wonder for the world.

> I took away how magical our world is: trees, woods, nature. When life is stressful, being in the woods, feeling the unity and power of nature, can help dissolve the stress in your life. I felt awe, and so happy and privileged to be here with them, immersed in their energy.

Throughout the next decade, Pete continued to build treehouses as a side hustle, looking forward to the day that he could focus 100 percent on them. Finally in 2005, he started his slow transition to becoming "the Treehouse guy."

Then, in 2008, he read *The Last Child in the Woods* by Richard Louv. At the time, he was hired by Longwood Gardens in Pennsylvania to build a temporary treehouse for an event that the author was participating in. Pete sat in the audience, and Louv's talk reinforced his mission and life path to nurture people's need to feel embraced by nature.

(The treehouse is still there, and this author has checked it out!)

Pete's dream really was cemented when he was approached by the TV channel Animal Planet. His show, called *Treehouse Masters,* recently wrapped its eleventh and final season.

> It was clear to the show executives that the treehouse wasn't "it." It was the story *behind* the treehouse. The childhood dream turned real. My clients often cry when they see it done, and every time, I do, too. I understand the power of these spaces. It's very cathartic.

In addition, he and his wife, Judy, have created a bed-and-breakfast property outside of Seattle with seven treehouses.

> I get to see people's response to these magical spaces in the trees! I always ask them, how well did you sleep? And without fail, people say, "Oh my gosh, I slept like a rock!"

Can you imagine spending the night in a treehouse?

> I'm putting people directly into the arms of nature. I am following my bliss, and I am so grateful for that. We are in this together. Being in the woods, nature, gives you a chance to recognize this reality.

And, of course, we couldn't end this story without mentioning the fate of those amazing, magnificent trees. Yes, they were saved. Thanks to a deal struck by California Senator Dianne Feinstein, Luna, and others, they are now part of the nonprofit Sanctuary Forest.

"To the trees! To the trees!" is Pete's famous line.

What Is It about Trees?

Trees draw in those that are willing to hear their message. It's as if they have their antennae out, looking for their next target. I think you know what I mean.

I do believe that trees call to all of us, everyone. And we can hear them or not. It's our choice.

As children many of us were open enough to hear them.

They invited us to climb up and hang from the branches. We would sit up high and gain a new perspective of our neighborhood.

We were naturally drawn to trees. We'd sit there and imagine we were on a mountain, or at the top of a castle, looking down on our kingdom. We rested underneath, looking up at the sway of leaves and sun.

We were playful in the trees. We played with the trees. Some of us even spoke with the trees, as if they were friends, because we knew that they were.

Being so close and intimate with these nature beings is one of the joys of childhood!

But then we were indoctrinated into the Western mindset that we were not only separate from nature, but we were in charge. Trees became nothing more than a resource, or worse, a nuisance in the way of progress.

But some of us never believed those lies. We have kept our tree friends close. We feel the joy of connection and playfulness. We feel the sharp pang of a chainsaw, as if we were the ones being assaulted.

We created a relationship with many trees. In fact, I would bet my life savings that you have a special tree friend, either on your property or in a local park. Maybe it's a tree you encountered once, or every day. Perhaps you are sitting within its view *right now*.

Why do we have this love of trees?

Some trees are "mother" trees. They nourish and support many trees in their surrounding area. They have huge energy fields, and some people can even *see* them. I wish I could. Perhaps one day I will.

However, I can *feel* the field, or aura. And you might be able to as well. We may be aware of it at times, but often, we are not. We just know that sitting by or under a tree makes us feel better.

One interesting study that I stumbled upon tracked how the flow tree sap altered itself to match a meditator's breath when sitting with it. Pretty remarkable! Trees seemed to be consciously entraining with their guests.

The trees that catch your attention are calling out to you. They want you to step into their field, to have an exchange, even for a brief moment.

They call to us when we see their bountiful or stark beauty. They call to us in the day and at night. They call to us every season and every storm.

The other night we had a rare "winter storm" that brought two inches of rain and sixty-mile-per-hour gusts. In essence, it was a tropical storm. The worst of the storm was just after I got into bed. Our house is surrounded by thirty maple and oak trees, roughly seventy to eighty feet tall.

And the wind howled. You would hear the trees being battered by the gusts. And I can now say, without hesitation, that I felt their stress, their roots holding on to water-soaked soil.

A while later, we felt a thud. We jumped out of bed, running to each window, hoping that no trees had come down. Thankfully, it was just a large branch that had fallen on our lawn. But I had so much adrenaline in my body that it took me a few hours to fall asleep. I felt the consciousness of those trees. The storm subsided.

Trees hold a presence within them—a consciousness—but humanity has grown numb to their existence. In the desolate places we recognize, ravaged by industry, the spirit of nature has fled. The land, once nurtured by their presence, is no longer sustained.

We must call the spirits back to help heal the land. This is a central part of my work as an earth energy healer, but it's something everyone can and must contribute to. By reading and engaging with the practices in this book, you are already playing your part.

Last week, while walking along a trail with no one around, I stopped to connect to a large tulip tree. They are the hugest trees in this part of Long Island, with leaves that are shaped like tulips. (Interestingly, they are called tulip trees due to those tulip-shaped flowers that bud in spring!)

I asked the tree for permission to connect and for any messages that it wanted to share. Suddenly, not a minute later, there was a foghorn blast in the harbor! It was startling how immediately that horn sounded.

I read that as a message of warning from the nature spirits. As I mentioned in the introduction, we are living in urgent times, and nature will reach out to share this message often and loudly, to whomever will listen.

Trees can serve as a reflection of our emotions and psyche. Just as Itzhak shares in this sacred story of his childhood.

> "Perhaps it also serves as a reminder of my strength,
> a metaphor for who I am now:, a shamanic healer."
>
> —Itzhak Beery

The Lonely Tree

Itzhak Beery grew up in an Israeli kibbutz on the slopes of Mount Gilboa. The mountain is known as the place where King Saul took his own life after his three sons were slain during the battle with the Philistines. It was later cursed by Saul's successor, King David, who lamented his fallen King. Mount Gilboa was to "have no dew or rain or fields for offerings"—as inscribed in the Bible—an homage to this terrible defeat.

In Itzhak's childhood, the mountain (actually a ridge) remained faithful to the curse. It was a barren, rocky landscape, consisting only of hard rock, heavy soil, and dry thorns. Although it was just under 1,700 feet, it dominated the eastern Jezreel Valley, which is three hundred feet below sea level.

The mountain has always served as a point of reference in the landscape, like a compass. It was impossible to get lost if it was in sight.

But at this time, there were no roads on the mountain. It was immutable and virginal.

> But one morning, I was stunned to see bulldozers cutting in the live flesh of the mountain. They came into our little corner of the world, sent by the government to build a snaking road to the top of the ridge. I'm unsure if I was the only one, but I felt that this powerful mountain was being desecrated. I could feel her pain in my little body as if I were being excavated. Her roads were my scars.

But despite the barren landscape, one lone tree managed to grow and survive. It dominated the mountain's skyline, visible from the kibbutz and the valley below. One tree. It was called the Sidra or Dom. A thorny desert tree with small, sweet, yellowish-orange plum-like fruits.

> For me, the Sidra was like a lighthouse, majestically overlooking the valley. Like a shaman, commanding and watching with its lonesome, mysterious powers of observation.

As with many spiritual traditions, trees have always served as a place of prayer in the ancient Hebrew tradition. Before organized religion, there were no houses of prayers like synagogues, mosques, or temples. They worshipped at altars constructed at the base of trees. Any tree. Before modern Judaism, God *was* the tree. The Hebrew word for God—El—is reflected in the name of two significant trees.

The indigenous Hebrews believed in male and female gods: El and Ela. They are the two sides of God. God and Shekhinah. Like the Alon and Ela trees, which stand side-by-side. In Kabbalah, the wisdom base of everything is the Tree of Life or the Tree of Knowledge.

The archetype of the tree represents who we are and what we aspire to be. A tree with strong roots possesses a solid foundation in a nurturing earth. Branches reaching toward the sun mimic our connection to the Divine.

Trees are a sacred symbol for most of the world's religions. We look to trees for wisdom, such as the Bodhi Tree which Siddhartha Gautama, known as the Buddha, sat against and was enlightened.

Mother trees—world trees—are worshipped in the jungles, deserts, flatlands, and mountaintops alike.

Within the last few hundred years we have changed our relationship with trees. Over generations, we have nearly severed the relationship.

In this modern era, we mostly see trees as a resource, as separate from us and lacking any consciousness. We have destroyed the altars of earth-based faiths and replaced them with manmade structures.

So now, when we cut down trees in the Amazon, it breaks our hearts. It's not just a tree. It's a whole community of life that suffers. Just as I felt as a young boy.

In the kibbutz, it was common practice to house the children separately to sleep. Itzhak would lie in his bed, fearful of sheer darkness and night sounds from wild animals, such as coyotes. Then there were the snakes, scorpions, and lizards who worked their way inside. In those houses, they were completely exposed and vulnerable; without an adult by his side, he felt unprotected.

For him, this lone tree on the mountain was a beacon of life. Although it was in a most inhospitable place, it was precisely that environment that caused it to be a place of life.

> The thorny desert tree had attracted an abundance of wildlife, including deer. They retreated from the heat-punishing daylight to rest in the shade, under its wide canopy.
>
> The deer would join the tree in watching over the valley.
>
> I identified with that tree. There were times I felt so lonely in that kibbutz. I didn't belong. But for some reason, I did, just like that tree.

The climb up was challenging, even dangerous, and still is. Itzhak and the other children would rest under the shade of the leaves and have an apple or two and count the random tiny cars on the road below. But their favorite part was the thrill of running back down to the kibbutz, full throttle, through hard soil and rock, propelled by the gravity of the steep incline.

Eventually, Itzhak moved away and then to New York, where he still resides. He left his childhood behind. He went into advertising and started his firm. But around the age of forty, as with many seekers, he felt the need to reflect and started asking the big questions. "Who am I? What is the purpose of my life?"

In the process, he felt a pull back to Israel to explore his roots. He discovered that a great grandfather had been a Kabbalistic rabbi and healer in Poland.

Around this time, my oldest son lived in Israel, so I decided to join him for a week. I felt the need to see my childhood home again with him. He was in his early twenties, and I wanted him to meet the tree that shaped my life.

When they reached the kibbutz, it was chilly late in the afternoon. The sun was getting ready to set over the ridge on their trek up. When they reached the tree, Itzhak felt a tinge of disappointment, as often happens when revisiting a place as an adult. The tree, which seemed to dominate this slope, was in actuality only about ten feet tall. It was more like a bush than the dominating tree he recalls from his youth.

Nevertheless, it still provided ample shade. They sat under the tree, while Itzhak recounted stories from his childhood. But then, the most magical thing happened.

> There are some deer that live in this area, but they are like ghosts. We often see their droppings but rarely encounter them. At this moment, with my son, a family of four deer just showed up. I suppose they came there to eat or for shelter, or both.
>
> But when they saw us there, unmoving, they didn't scare away and seemed to accept our presence. We watched them silently in awe as the sun set and the vibrant changing colors of the landscape spread before us. It was something that we will never forget.

So, then what did they do?

> I was almost fifty, but we had to run down the slope, screaming and laughing like I did as a child! As I was galloping down the steep slope, my knee made a cracking sound, and I fell. I managed to damage my meniscus. But that experience with my son was worth it.
>
> My own experience was unique, but I now realized that anyone that lives within proximity to mountains, trees, rivers, oceans, deserts, in their early childhood, develops an intimate

relationship with it. It's part of their identity imprinted in their souls.

Mount Gilboa served as my compass. The Sidra tree was a metaphor for my lonely but reflective childhood, not feeling like I belonged, but belonging nevertheless. Perhaps it also serves as a reminder of my strength, a metaphor for who I am now: a shamanic healer that hopefully provides respite, shade, and sweet fruits to nourish those in need.

All This Talk about Trees

I think many of us can relate to Itzhak's experience with his tree. During times of pain, we can develop deep relationships with trees. They can nurture our souls. They may appear solitary creatures—and they are like we are—but just like us, they are all connected, sharing their consciousness.

In the last few years, there has been lots of talk about how trees and plants communicate with each other and the vast fungal network underground which doubles as the largest living organism on Earth.

There is much research about the sentience of plants and how they respond to changes in their environment. How forests are a collective, dependent, and cooperative community rather than individual, independent beings competing for resources.

And who among us has not conversed with a tree, especially in childhood? I would climb up into the maple tree in my backyard when I needed space and time alone. I was able to see my neighbor's acre lot, which was wild and unkempt, according to the standards of suburbia. Rather than a new ranch, like the others in our 1960s development, it was an old, dusty farmhouse whose land, at one time, must have encompassed our parcel as well as others in the surrounding area.

I would sit up in my tree, camouflaged by the leaves. Although I was only twenty feet from the back door, no one could see me. I remember the taste of her leaves even now. The strength of her branches. The stability of her trunk as I climbed up.

I found peace in her embrace.

Most of us have a story to share about a favorite tree in our childhood. Sometimes there are amazing stories of kinship with a tree or a forest. There are mythological stories of tree beings, like Yggdrasil, the mythical tree in Norse mythology, or the Tree of Life in Kabbalah. Many indigenous cultures talk about the spirits that inhabit trees and many of the world's religions worshipped trees, such as oak and ash, and held prayer and ceremony in groves of trees.

Jean Shinoda Bolen posits, in her book *Like a Tree*, that there are "tree people" and "non-tree people." I believe that she is partly right. I believe that the non-tree people are really "those-that-forgot-they-were-tree-people." They lost touch with their imagination and wonder. And now they are disconnected from the magic and mystery of trees.

Tree hugging has become popular at spiritual retreats, and people absolutely love it! I believe it's because participants are finally given permission to do what they truly desire—without fear of judgment.

Yet, in public, we often feel awkward about it.

Not only do we crave this connection, but I've found that trees do too. They tell me how often they are ignored, seen merely as physical objects devoid of consciousness. But nothing could be further from the truth. Trees have unique personalities and profound wisdom.

Many of the stories shared during my interviews reflect a deep emotional bond with trees—how they can inspire awakening and serve as initiators of personal transformation. Our connection with trees can mark a pivotal moment, changing the trajectory of our lives.

Below is a story of how our attention, and relationship seeking, can impact the trees in our lives.

> "Places that are easy to get to often call out to you
> a little more."
>
> —Josh Heath

The Dying Tree

Josh Heath was around ten years old, building forts in his family's front yard, when his father suggested that he move his activity to the backyard. "In fact," his dad said, "build it in the silver maple behind the garage. It's dying anyway."

It was true, the large eighty-foot tree had passed its prime. Nothing that they could do would damage it any more than it already was.

The tree was part of their property in rural Maine that his parents bought from his grandparents in September of 1985. They were hours from the closest city of any kind, and four hours to Boston. Finding wilderness was easy.

The tree was part of a rundown spot where old, rusted car parts and bramble took over. Since it wasn't viewable from the house, it was a perfect place to build a secret fort.

The tree was actually an ornamental poplar, with dark green and gray leaves soft to the touch, turning darkish yellow in the fall and then brown and crunchy in the winter. The trunk had deeply furrowed bark at the bottom that was smooth higher up with the newer growth. Unlike poplars, and most trees in the forest, this one had room to grow. Its wide canopy and strong limbs made it a dream to climb.

So that summer, Josh was joined by his cousins, Jason and TJ, and several neighborhood friends to build a proper fort. After surveying the half-dead tree, they grabbed hacksaws and axes and proceeded to prune it. They cut back dead branches and cleared the ground around its base.

Once complete, they now had a blank slate, a fresh start.

Those long, hot summer days were spent lugging wood from his neighbor's yard. Mr. Collins was a shed-builder for a local lumber company and offered his scraps, which were the perfect size for the project.

They used a variety of tools all taken from their garages and tool sheds, not really knowing what they were doing. Handfuls of nails, assorted hammers, and saws. No one advised them on how to build, nor did they seek advice.

The fathers and older neighbors knew. Keep them busy and out of trouble in these vulnerable preteen years.

They built the fort at the base of the tree. The main room, probably nine by four feet, was the central gathering place. The two-foot-wide tree trunk was at the center of this space. They cobbled together a tin roof and finished with old shingles.

As they spent hours with this tree every day, they became intimate with it. Intimate in a way that you know the curves and knots, the smell and touch of every aspect of it. So, it didn't take long for Josh and his friends to notice changes in this tree. Suddenly they became aware that the tree was sprouting again. Where there was dead wood, now new shoots and leaves were bursting to life.

Josh's dad suggested that the tree must have needed the iron from all those nails they hammered in. The iron in the nails, perhaps, brought the tree back to life, not unlike taking vitamins and supplements for well-being.

Now, at forty-one years old, with extensive education on trees, Josh realizes that tree was probably root bound and stagnant. The pruning of branches stimulated new growth. It allowed the tree to breathe. A perfectly logical and scientific reality.

But more than this, Josh realizes the deeper metaphor of what occurred. They turned their attention to the tree. They pruned it and gave it care. They brought life, laughter, and joy where there had been decades of stagnation and neglect. They literally brought the spirit of the tree back to life!

Over the next few years, they built additions to the tree house, added ropes from the branches, and staked their claim with a flag made from a piece of tin.

This was their place. They would hang out in and around this fort nearly every day for about five years. They would steal peas from the nearby garden in the summertime. They spent countless hours using this fort in all seasons. Playing hide and seek, telling stories.

> It was our refuge where our sense of imagination could run wild. There was no limit put on the creativity that this place instilled in all of us.

Josh even remembers the smell of the wood. Spicy. Ornamental trees have a spicy scent, like cinnamon and nutmeg, when it's living wood. Once harvested with an axe, the wood becomes orange and pungent and stringy—"it's a son of a bitch to split."

As a child, leaning up against the tree, Josh felt a sense of welcoming. Only now, he realizes that the tree was responding to him and his friends. It embraced their project with feelings of warmth and acceptance. It was inviting them into relationship. In contrast, there was another tree on his property. Every time they attempted to climb it, big winds would kick up. Josh and his friends finally stayed away.

Over the years, after joining high school sports and then going away to college, the fort went unused and eventually needed to be torn down.

Josh now realizes the importance of that place, not just for his youthful teen adventures, but more importantly, in helping to ground him and teach him how to process situations in life.

> That tree was always a place I'd go when things were bugging me. I'd climb into the tree, about forty feet in the air. We built a few wood seats high up in the canopy. I'd go there and sit. It was a place to be vulnerable, where I could cry. Sometimes it would take my mom a half hour to find me.

In college, Josh took a journaling class on perspectives on nature. On the 150-acre campus, most of his friends would go out into the forest to complete the exercises. Josh observed the pine grove right outside his dorm window. Proximity doesn't matter, he realized.

> Back then, if you asked me, I would've said that I was going to be a park ranger or game warden. But I see now how the experience with that tree gave me a foundational connection to nature, and with trees, specifically. When I was introduced to forest bathing, the concept fell into place so easily for me. I realized that I had been doing it my whole life.

Nowadays, Josh is a forest therapy guide, and talks about mindfulness in nature.

> The biggest thing that I tell everyone that comes to my forest bathing walks, or comes to a class, is that we don't need to go to Colorado, Finland, or Australia to have a profound nature experience. We can have it in our own backyard. No excuses.
>
> I'm sitting seventy yards from my house right now, in a place that I call my sit spot. Places that are easy to get to often call out to you a little more.
>
> Even when I outgrew the fort, I never outgrew the spot and that tree.

As part of his work, Josh sometimes visits New York City. He talked about a forest bathing walk he did in Riverside Park, in upper Manhattan.

> I grew up in rural Maine. Vast expanses of nature were outside my door. But grow up on 195th Street in New York City, with the concrete and pavement, noise, lights, and hustle? Nature seems so far away. But I was blown away by the peace and calm that we connected with in that little park on the Hudson River.

Josh feels strongly that we need to fall in love with something—form an intimate connection to it—to be able to care for and be a steward for it. We need relationship.

Josh finishes his story with, "That tree in my childhood was the beginning of this journey I'm on. It was the setup for my greater appreciation and love of nature. Ultimately, it was an early sign of who I am and what I do today."

Josh and his friends gave attention and love to that tree and the tree was revived. It flourished. Then the tree, in turn, awakened Josh to the path that he continues to live today: awakening others to the magic of nature.

Trees can awaken us to the reciprocity of experience. And sometimes, they give us messages to relay to others, who are no longer listening. A friend, Bonnie, shares how she was given a message and the sheer realization that she could hear it!

> "Doubts of my connection with nature vanished.
> Only certainty remained."
>
> —Bonnie Casamassima

Awakened by a Tree

Bonnie Casamassima spent the most recent decade in both the academic and corporate worlds researching and analyzing how our spaces impact our well-being and quality of life. She worked roughly sixty to seventy hours a week.

> To say that my life was out of balance is an understatement. It was ironic that my work sought to improve people's lives and well-being, yet I was so in need of that myself.

Over the course of a few years, Bonnie had a series of "awakenings" to her spiritual side, and one such awakening led her to enroll in a yearlong shamanic training in the summer of 2021.

During the first weekend of the training, they were given a simple assignment: Go outside into the yard and see what happens. See what draws your attention. Just go with the flow.

Bonnie thought to herself, *Sounds pretty random. What's this about?* Her overactive, analytical mind was stirred.

Bonnie joined the other ten participants and walked out the door to a shining sun. It was a hot June day.

There was the sound of shamanic drumming in the yard, as two guests were leading a rhythmic beat that is known to induce a trance-like state.

> Almost immediately, one oak tree drew my attention. I suddenly felt a warmth, a fire stirring within my heart, a sort of magnet that pulled me to the tree. I felt the words *Come sit with me.*

Her rational mind kept trying to pull her back. In her head, she wondered, *Is this real?*

> But it's almost like I couldn't talk myself out of approaching that tree. I started breathing into the moment as I got closer.

She instinctively knelt down in front of the oak and closed her eyes. Only now she realizes that she was somehow mimicking the posture for approaching the sacred.

> I felt a sort of giving away of the soil beneath my legs. I no longer felt the weight of my body. It was as if I was hovering, weightless, yet grounded and supported. It was as if I was part of the earth, the ground.
>
> Suddenly, a conversation telepathically popped into my head. Everything else faded around me. The yard, the other participants, even the drumming was softer, as if it was coming

from over the hill. I was in this bubble with the tree—just the two of us.

Words entered the upper right part of my head, the part that is associated with creativity, imagination, and intuition. It then filled my whole body. I felt that warmth again, that fire, which overcame my heart.

The only distraction from her experience were the mosquitos, and, of course, that old reliable, rational mind.

"Do you really want to hear this?" it said. When I found myself really trying hard to be present, I would surrender to the flow. Thankfully, my curiosity and heart-center won out.

Words popped into her head...and she knew there weren't hers. They were coming *through* her.

The tree said that it was craving human attention and relationship, and was so grateful for our connection. It was exciting to be seen by another! Although it wasn't one of the big trees in the landscape, it was grateful, as a "secondary" tree, to capture my notice.

The tree went on to say that it really loves being in the wooded land of this family's home. It asked Bonnie to tell the homeowners that it loves that the children play in the yard and bring joy and light. Joy is the language of trees!

Then the tree shared a message for me and others. Trees are both hard with their exterior bark, while at the same time being flexible to facilitate growth and expansion. That growth comes from within.

That message landed strongly for her. It was about the harmony of opposites, known as yin and yang. As Bonnie struggled with a decade-long focus on the material world, her spiritual being had been subjugated, unable to grow and express itself.

In the past, she had dismissed her experiences of intuitive knowing and a deep sensitivity to spirit and nature, because she, like many of us, was taught to undervalue nonrational thought.

She saw those aspects, which lead to greater wholeness, as a weakness. The feminine (softness, openness, and receptivity) can be experienced while also inhabiting aspects of the masculine (strength, boundaries, and discernment).

> My experience with that oak was a sacred gift. It was pure love and heart connection. Any doubts that I had about the invisible realm of our human experience were gone. Doubts of my connection to nature vanished. Only certainty remained.
>
> I left that day, knowing both in my head and my heart, that I was following the right path. The question of, "Who am I? A medium or an academic professor?" was gone. My identity can and will inhabit both spheres. This is the total me. The wholeness that I never felt before.

We can feel a tremendous depth of connection to tree beings. This relationship may come from childhood or can go back even further than that. Our tree connection may be ancestral. A connection that flows in our veins, written into our DNA, carried across the ages.

"Wherever they took axes to its trunk, blood poured out."

—Faith Adiele

Ancestral Resonance

When I started to interview Faith Adiele for this book, the synchronicities started immediately. She shared that she was suddenly getting a lot of pitches by magazines to write about places in nature. Then my request for an interview came through.

Faith shares, "My tagline is 'I don't like nature.' I'm an indoor cat. I would never choose to be in nature. But I am a travel writer. So why is this happening?"

I thought, *how curious*. She chose a career that requires her to be in nature so much of the time. And even more than that, both her parents were raised in rural villages—her mother in the Pacific Northwest, her father in Southeastern Nigeria.

> Well, I was always outside as a child. I was raised by my Nordic mother and grandparents on a small farm. My grandparents were outdoorsy and always took me camping, horseback riding, and fishing. My summers were often spent in a trailer or cabin, out in the wilderness. I have fond memories of that time in my life.
>
> But after my grandparents passed away, and I left for college, I realized that my race, my Blackness, determined how I was perceived and where I felt welcome. I moved to the city, became more urban. Life was more about survival, and I closed off that side of me.

But Faith's story is about trees, and a surprising connection and resonance.

First, we spoke about a tree in her father's village.

Faith met her father for the first time in 1990, when she received a scholarship to attend graduate school in Nigeria. Her father was a professor at the University of Nigeria and had three other children. For the first time, Faith was no longer an only child.

But it took a while for Faith's father to drum up the courage to take her to his ancestral village.

> He didn't welcome me initially. We were living in the city. I think he needed to wait until Christmas, when, like in the US, everyone travels home. He knew the elders would be angry that he never told them about me, and I guess he thought they'd be more charitable during the holidays.

The ancestral village was an explosion of color. It had bright red soil and verdant green vegetation. Pastel-colored houses and a gigantic tree at the crossroads in the center of town.

Yes, this was the tree. At a crossroads. As Faith's understanding of her own life was at a crossroads. As her race was at a crossroads. As her life before and after this journey was at a crossroads.

The tree was so large that the branches cast shade over the entire square and people would sit on its roots like a bench.

During the Nigerian Civil War, Faith's father oversaw refugees who flooded into the area, fleeing the genocide. Finally, the Nigerian federal troops reached his town.

Toward the end of the war, it is said that the enemy saw this tree and—perhaps understanding its power as guardian—rushed to chop it down. Wherever they took axes to its trunk, blood poured out. The enemy fled in terror. The villagers respected this tree as a powerful protector.

In 2002, Faith returned with a PBS production crew to film a documentary about her family. The crew, also taken with the tree, made sure to film several sequences there. Faith spent quite a bit of time sitting under its branches, and she felt a strong, benevolent connection.

Around 2012, the village had fallen on hard times. While Faith was visiting, her sister told her that villagers had turned on the tree. Believing that it was causing them misfortune, they hacked away at the tree. Her sister warned Faith that now it was a fraction of its size. Unable to bear seeing the tree in this condition, Faith refused to visit it.

That same year, Faith was invited to an artist colony on an island in the Bahia region of Brazil. She intended to work on her book about finding her Nigerian family.

> I love Brazil. Africans were brought here hundreds of years ago, and I found out that many were of Nigerian descent. It was interesting to write about being Nigerian in the New World, where you could definitely see the existence of the culture here, more than in the US. Their African identity was alive.

On that trip, there were amazing, mystical happenings throughout her time there. The workers found out she was of Nigerian ancestry and invited her to come with them in the middle of the night to witness ancestral ceremonies in the forest.

> Here I am at three in the morning, hopping into a car to go deep into the forest. There are people dressed in masquerades, covered entirely from head to toe, who became vessels for the ancestors. They spoke Yoruba and practiced traditions I recognized from my time in Nigeria.
>
> One afternoon, I heard a knock at my door, asking if I would like to visit the ruins of the church in an old fishing village. It was one of the first Catholic churches in Brazil, built by the Jesuits in the mid-1500s. It was one of the first places where the explorer Amerigo Vespucci landed.

The church was set on fire twice by an indigenous priestess, but the Jesuits rebuilt it each time.

But eventually a big tree burst through the walls, simultaneously destroying and holding up the church. Tendrils covered the walls and windows, branches were breaking down the walls, and its trunk shot through the roof like a skyscraper.

> As soon as I saw the tree, I recognized it. I don't know the varieties of plants, but somehow, I knew this tree. It was so familiar.

As she wandered through the site, her host recounted the history of the church, when they saw two local women enter with bags.

> These women were placing something into the rubble of the walls. When I approached, I saw that it was broken Catholic figurines and melted candles. They said this consecrated ground is where they can safely dispose of the blessed statues.
>
> I asked them, "Do you know the name of this tree?" They didn't, but they knew the name of the spirit living within it: "Iroko."
>
> This was the name of the spirit of the tree in my father's village!
>
> I later researched the two tree genera. Though the Nigerian tree, which is the largest hardwood in Western Africa, and the Brazilian tree are two entirely different types of trees. They both house Iroko spirits, the gods of prosperity and fortune.
>
> It turns out this was the sacred tree of Candomblé, the fusion of Yoruba religion and Roman Catholicism and native shamanism, but I didn't know that! Somehow, I recognized the spirit.

Faith saw an amazing metaphor uniting colonized people. The Africans were enslaved in this country for five hundred years, the life span of this Iroko tree. When the colonizing church was rebuilt twice after a Tupinambá priestess destroyed it, the Africans' ancestral Iroko tree banded with the native people to finally take it down.

And even though the Nigerian people were forced to adapt in this new country, just like this tree, their indomitable spirit lives on.

Invitation: Connecting to a Tree

Start simple. Go for a walk among trees. Don't have a destination in mind. Just start walking and following your feet and see where they lead you. Look at the trees as you pass and see where you feel curious.

Want to touch the bark of that unusual tree? Is it smooth? Wrinkled with deep folds? Moss growing on one side?

Did you notice some squirrels suddenly ascending the trunk of a tree? Is the sun shining through the branches of a tree?

Whatever catches your attention, stop and notice. Observe. Look at the tree's branches. The leaves or fruit. What do you notice about the branches? Are they graceful or rigid? Does the tree look healthy or is it nearing the end?

Now, rub the palms of your hands gently and then hold them out a few inches from the trunk. Ask the tree for permission to connect. You may get a clear indication of a response either way. Or not.

Stay there for a few minutes. Do you notice any heat or tingling sensation in your palms? Close your eyes or keep them soft. Do you see anything unusual—any sounds, colors, shapes?

Are you getting any impressions or feeling any sensations in your body?

Invitation: "Become a Tree"

Find a tree that you would like to connect with through the genius of imagination. Ask for permission to connect. If you feel any hesitance or get any sign, with any of your senses, that the answer is no, move on to another tree. Any other reaction, and you are free to connect.

Sit at the base of the tree with your spine against the trunk. Get comfortable enough to be in this space for at least ten to fifteen minutes.

Slow your breath—inhale, exhale. You may eventually feel your breath entrain with the energy of the tree.

Using your imagination, you can imagine becoming very small and sinking into the soil, feeling what it's like to be in the roots. Engage your senses of sight, smell, texture, taste, and sound. Perhaps you may encounter some worms or other insects in the soil.

Now imagine yourself moving up through the trunk, following the path of water intake from the roots. Again, engage your senses.

Eventually, imagine finding yourself in one of the leaves. Feel the sunlight, oxygen, and exchange of nutrients.

Feel what it's like to be a tree. To be *this* tree. In this place.

If you have a question that you are looking for some guidance on, perhaps pose it. Be very observant of any possible answer that may come to you, either in the physical world (a breeze, squirrels running around, etc.) or in the imaginal realm, in the form of thoughts, words, or images which may arise.

When you feel complete with the response, see if the tree has a request from you. The request could be to visit this tree more often or to bring an offering on your next visit. It could be anything at all.

Slowly, make your way out of the tree, back into your body.

Give gratitude and thanks for the connection. And slowly open your eyes. Take some time before you arise. Be sure your energy is completely returned and whole in your body. You can do this by patting your arms, legs, and torso with your hands, and stamping your feet.

CHAPTER 5

Close Encounters with the Wild

~

"...there is a mysterious third world, the shared habitat of the heart. This is the deep connection between a person and another animal. It is the permeability of empathy. It is the connection that extends from within us, across the mysterious between, and into the other being. If we're lucky, we feel something almost indescribable in return. We can learn to enter this habitat at will. This transportive leap can change our lives and the lives around us for the better."

—**Richard Louv,** *Our Wild Calling: How Connection with Animals Can Transform Our Lives and Save Theirs*

~

Following Alabaster

Our daily lives include encounters with wildlife. From a hawk soaring overhead while we drive to a chipmunk scampering across the lawn. And depending on where we live, we may have daily encounters with larger mammals.

But unusual encounters are something else. A bird flies into your open car when you run into the house for a forgotten wallet. A coyote walks past you on a deserted beach. These are not our typical daily experiences.

These encounters stir an ancient, primitive connection deep within us. We look into the eyes of an animal and somehow, we can connect. We can feel their fear, their pain, or their curiosity.

For all of time, humans have had these relationships with animals. Many indigenous traditions believe in spirit or power animals—personal protectors and guides that embody a specific animal species. They bring us wisdom from other realms. Interpreting the meaning of the animal's physical qualities and behavior is said to give us insight into their wisdom and relevance in our lives.

We can have an animal spirit guide for our entire lives, and we can also have ones that come into our lives during a transitional period to help us through. Spirit animals can show up in our dreams or everyday life. They may even come to us in a ceremony, such as a shamanic drumming journey, where participants are brought into a theta consciousness, not unlike a dreamlike state.

When people learn about spirit animals, they sometimes realize that, indeed, they have had a strong connection with a particular species since childhood. And that they resonate with the teachings that this animal embodies.

Spirit animals can come in the guise of an eagle, snake, or wolf. They can be as big as a whale or as tiny as an inchworm.

And it doesn't need to be an exotic encounter with living beings either. Even the most common animal making an appearance in our lives can call us to attention, to listen and be still.

When my grandmother was nearly ninety years old, she would sit by the window and watch the wildlife outside. When I visited her, she would tell me about the squirrels and the birds visiting our yard. I used to think, *Geez, is this what I have to look forward to?*

But now I've gotten older (and "wiser") and yes, it is truly something to "look forward to." We installed a birdfeeder across from the kitchen sink. We love watching the parade of wildlife in our backyard. I downloaded a free bird identification app on my phone and use it all the time to learn about the names, calls, and behaviors of the birds visiting our yard.

Recent findings from the German Center for Integrative Biodiversity Research show that greater bird diversity brings greater joy to people.

Two years ago, when trying to be more observant of nature, my husband and I noticed a black squirrel, which is rare among Long Island's gray squirrel population. Once we noticed him, it was hard not to see him as an individual. We watched as he moved around our yard, building a nest, playing with others, collecting nuts.

Then, one day, we noticed him with babies, and he was a "she." I named her Alabaster, because I'm silly. But it was thrilling to see how Alabaster moved out of her nest when our neighbor took down a nearby tree. The next day, she carried her babies, in her teeth, one by one across our yard and driveway to her new nest across the street from our house.

I learned that squirrel mommas have multiple nests in the area just in case.

One of her babies was black, too. It was wonderful to watch as they grew and quickly went off on their own.

With spontaneous encounters, there is a magic of synchronicity. Why did that red tail hawk swoop down just over my car as I headed down to the beach? Why did I find that baby seal on the side of the road in February? What about the huge spider, spinning her web just outside my door?

Swiss psychologist Carl G. Jung would say that these are indeed synchronicities. Rather than just happenstance, their presence is perfectly synced to intersect in our lives.

And, as Hobie shares in this next story, these synchronicities are often metaphoric messages to help us on our journey in life.

Winter in Yellowstone

"It was an *'Oh, shit!'* moment. What do I do?"

—Hobie Hare

As someone who grew up in the South, Hobie always had a fascination with winter. On the rare occasion that it snowed in Richmond, VA, his world came alive. With sledding, making snow people, building snow forts. When he decided on graduate school, he made his way to the School for International Training in Brattleboro, VT, for a master's in teaching, where he enjoyed the full winter experience.

Just after 9/11, he had been a National Park Service ranger, working season to season in Yellowstone. Unsure of his next gig, he got a call from his supervisor's colleague asking if he'd be available to work as an interpretive ranger that winter at Fishing Bridge in Yellowstone National Park.

Without hesitation, he said yes! Mostly because he needed the work, but also because it meant being in the heart of Yellowstone's interior over the winter, which he had not yet experienced.

Soon after accepting, he realized the full extent of what the position demanded. He'd be over fifty miles from the nearest paved road, living with a small community of just twenty people in government housing near Yellowstone Lake. To prepare, he had to haul gear, clothes, provisions, and other necessities for the next three months on a sled attached to a snowmobile. He couldn't help but wonder: *Am I in over my head?*

> But it ended up being an extremely magical winter where my creativity, my sense of wonder, and my creative self-expression were reignited because everything was stripped away—everything was so refreshingly elemental. I had to get down to the basics in order to thrive in this remote environment.

It was just before the Winter Solstice, less than two weeks after he arrived at Yellowstone Lake.

> I was returning back home after a full day at the Canyon Area warming hut. At the time, the hut was a glorified double-wide trailer that served as part concession stand with hot drinks, snacks, and sandwiches, and part nature, travel, and safety education clearinghouse for winter visitors traveling through the area.

He drove his snowmobile slowly heading south. He had made it safely through the isolated, windswept Hayden Valley and was nearing home at Fishing Bridge by the shore of Yellowstone Lake. He was approaching the Mud Volcano thermal area, which tends to attract bison, especially in the colder months.

It was near dusk, with maybe thirty minutes of light remaining. He'd done this commute a few times since he arrived and was comfortable with the timing and path. The road was snow packed with big drifts on either side and the ice-covered Yellowstone River flowed just beyond that to the east.

> As I was rounding a curve, looming before me about fifty feet away, a big bull bison was standing in the middle of the road. Just him and me. I immediately stopped my engine. He was positioned in such a way that I couldn't go to the left side, near his face with his huge head and horns, nor go to the right, toward his back end because he could kick or trample me.
>
> I thought, *How amazing that this animal is built for this landscape and this life. Maybe I am, too.* I'm about to find out.

Yellowstone is one of the last refuges for this magnificent animal to roam free.

> I thought, *This guy could probably sit here all night and not die of starvation or hypothermia.* But I could not do so. I would have to move at some point.

Hobie had to stop. Be patient. Yet he couldn't wait all day.

It was so early in the season that he wasn't quite sure how to handle the encounter. His training hadn't prepared him for this moment. People were often advised to slow down and let the bison make the first move, so that became his plan.

> I certainly wouldn't want him to waste his energy as every ounce of fat is critical to their survival at this time of year.

Unlike a lot of people in such an encounter, Hobie seemed to be as concerned about this animal as he was about himself.

Hobie explains the winter challenges of bison. Depending on weather conditions, ice storms and freezing rain mixed with snow layers may make it impossible for them to reach the grass to eat closer to the ground. One such winter, in 1997, there was a mass die-off of bison in the region due to starvation.

Ironically, the road itself was the path of least resistance. It was groomed enough to help the bull bison travel while conserving his energy. Just as it was for Hobie.

Hobie assumed a patient stance of observing and staying fully present.

> I saw his breath coming out from his face. Steam rising outward with each exhale. I was amazed at how massive and intimidating he was.

Hobie was completely vulnerable on a low seat of a snowmobile. He was completely exposed.

It was remarkably quiet with the snowmobile turned off. The wind blew gently through the trees and across the landscape, with soft snow falling and shimmering like diamonds.

It was at that moment that he was temporarily distracted by a large black raven coming from behind that flew low, just over his head.

> It was so low that I heard and felt the *whoosh, whoosh* of his wings.

It landed in some nearby trees, as if to join this observation party, to see what was going on.

Hobie looked up at the bird, and he could tell that the bison sensed it was there, too.

"There was this interesting thing going on. The raven was watching me. The bison was watching me. And all my energy and focus were on the bison's every movement." Hobie was careful to retain gentle eye contact with him as many large mammals interpret direct eye contact to be aggressive behavior. He casually observed the animal for signs of aggression, such as stomping his hooves or sticking his tail straight out.

After several minutes of watching each other—which felt like an eternity—the bison then started walking slowly toward Hobie, the soft-crunching sound of his hooves approaching on the snow.

Hobie recalls maintaining a peaceful, calm smile, as if the bison could read and respond to that unspoken cue.

In the brief encounter, this massive two-thousand-pound being, standing six feet tall at the shoulder, dominated his entire attention.

"It was an *'Oh, shit!'* moment. What do I do?" Bison can run up to thirty-five miles an hour. Yet he was still able to marvel at the power and grace the bull bison possessed in his movement.

His nose almost touched the front of his snowmobile, his body within inches of the skis on either side.

> I recall thinking, *Are my parents going to get a call that this was my last day on the planet?* But I had to remain calm. I recall moving my body slowly back a bit and to one side, giving myself a little more personal space.

He watched as the bison's chest was heaving up and down, not unlike his own. He realized that his own breath was in sync with this majestic animal. Inhaling, exhaling, low and deliberate, this elemental thing that we all share.

The bull seemed intentional, taking his time to check him out and weigh his options.

Then, he just maneuvered away a little bit, moving gradually toward a clearing between the trees.

When the bison was at a safer distance, Hobie turned on his snowmobile and slowly went past him.

> When I looked back, I could swear that his eyes were still locked on me. Two wild beings seeing each other.
>
> At that moment, the raven stirred from its perch, dropped within six feet of my head as he flew over, then landed in the nearby trees.

Hobie intuitively knew, from this encounter, that he would be okay in the wintertime wilderness. He'd be safe and looked after by nature.

> As long as I stayed observant, present, and in harmony with the surrounding environment, I would be alright.
>
> Thankfully, this space in my life afforded few distractions from the outside world. Limited cell phone and internet service. My creativity was ignited. It was a magical time. I was able to tap more deeply into my artistic self-expression and spend time on nature photography, writing, and finishing an outdoor program correspondence course that I was enrolled in.
>
> I was isolated and cocooned from the larger world, still grappling with the tragedy of 9/11 and what was to come after.
>
> Ultimately, the message that I received from this encounter was that I was not in charge. I needed to surrender, to yield to the massive power of nature. To slow down and be present. It inspired me to be more introspective in my life and my path. And it reinvigorated my childlike wonder, delight, and joy in nature, and my desire to lead a simplified life.
>
> It's interesting now that much of my guiding work in Yellowstone takes place in the winter months. The joy it brings me to witness this majestic place at such a magical time of year keeps me coming back.

Living in Yellowstone, and having the bison and raven encounter, helped him prepare to be open to the wonder of symbols and messages of the natural world.

> Yellowstone is a magical place for me. It encouraged me to be still, patient, and aware. It also taught me that not dealing with or facing situations that are so intense and challenging can also create stagnation. At some point, it didn't really matter what the step was, but I had to take a step forward. I didn't have to see or know where I was heading. The bison showed me that this world is truly magical. There is so much more delight, joy, and wisdom available if we only pay attention.

Hobie's encounter was shocking and potentially life-threatening. It was a magical story of spontaneous entrainment with the bison. They seemed to become one. Sometimes our encounters with other-than-human beings are gentle and accepting—something to remember as Janine shares her story.

> "Then a hushed silence as they went back to sleep."
>
> —Janine Benyus

A Kayak in Night Fog

Janine Benyus was staying solo in her small old miner's cabin on Georgetown Lake. At an elevation of 6,400 feet in Montana, she has a view of the twenty-four peaks of the Anaconda Mountain Range, surrounded by the Anaconda-Pintler Wilderness. This area is known for the largest US breeding population of red-necked grebes.

It was October and cold, but the lake hadn't frozen yet. Lots of waterfowl were migrating to their southern wintering range, but few people were around.

One night, Janine couldn't sleep and decided to take the kayak out.

> The lake air was milky with fog, which happens when the water is warmer than the night air. The fog was thick and there was a nearly full moon which was illuminating each fog particle, making the air a milky white.

In contrast, the lake water was dark, making her feel like she was in a black-and-white film. Janine paddled briskly across the lake to keep warm.

As she made her way into Jericho Bay, she spotted a huge group of sleeping migrating ducks as her kayak was poised to burst right into their peaceful sanctuary.

> I realized suddenly that my kayak would dive right into them at high speed! I immediately stopped paddling, held my breath and prayed, just as if I were poised to hit another car. And my momentum continued to draw me closer.

And as she got closer and got a broader view of the scene, she realized that there had to be four to five hundred ducks, grebes, geese, and coots in this group.

> I was horrified by what I was about to do! When migrating, the birds find sanctuary to feed and rest before their long journey south. Disrupting their rest could have tragic consequences, causing them to needlessly expend precious energy.
>
> But instead of suddenly fleeing at my presence, they just effortlessly parted in front of my boat and accepted me in. We were so close I could see their eyes watching me with curiosity. "What are you doing?" they seemed to say.

There was a quiet murmur among them, but that was it. Then a hushed silence as they went back to sleep.

I felt like I was in Eden, recalling a memory of being at one with nature. A place where there was no guilt for our modern trespasses on this planet. I felt like I belonged here, was accepted and welcomed. In fact, I felt that I was part of them.

I wanted to stay there and did for a while. They relaxed and eventually their proximity loosened up and I slowly, calmly backed myself out. It was as if we had an understanding. I wasn't going to harm them, and they seemed to know and trust that.

These moments remind me that we are on an extraordinary planet, and we somehow forget that.

The hushed silence is what we often recall so vividly in these encounters. The dark of night, or the dawn of early morning rising. Nicole shares a story of beauty and how much we have lost even if we think we are nature-connected.

> "I realized I was at the tip of the iceberg of my own awareness, and that I had no idea what was below that."
>
> —Nicole Craanen

I Thought I Was Connected to Nature

Nicole Craanen was always involved in nature. As a child, she spent a lot of time in the woods by her house and went camping with her family all around the US. But there is one story she keeps coming back to.

While camping with her husband, Nicole arose early, before the other campers started their day.

"I've been a meditator for about twenty years, and I thought, *I'll just sit out here and meditate.*" Which was something unusual, because she usually meditated in a center with a group of people or alone in her home.

She found her way to a picnic table, close to a bluff with expansive views. Suddenly, two turkey vultures flew about twenty feet away from her, opened their wings, and started pruning them.

> I had so many thoughts because, well, turkey vultures are kind of gross. They don't have feathers on their head. They eat carrion. They're not what we typically think of as beautiful birds. But there was something so incredible and majestic about being this close to these birds. They're massive. One of the biggest birds in North America.
>
> Sitting that close to them and watching them do this thing that felt somewhat vulnerable... While that was happening, a chipmunk scampered by my feet, taking no notice of me. I felt like Snow White!
>
> And I thought, *I've only been sitting here for twenty minutes quietly, and nature just erupted around me.* Like I was no longer in their space. I was just there. That gave me this moment of pause over how "people-y" the world is and how disruptive we are and how, if we're just quiet and we sit there, we have the ability to observe and be a part of.
>
> It was one of those pivotal experiences for me.

Nicole has done a lot of public speaking in the architecture and design community and started to incorporate nature walks into her talks when possible. She thought if taking walks is what got her to appreciate being in nature, then maybe that'll work for other people, too. "Maybe connecting them to nature will help them see how to build differently."

A couple years ago, she was certified as a forest bathing guide through the Association of Nature and Forest Therapy. Her training took place during Covid and was done virtually.

> It's funny because when I tell people I did it virtually, they're like, "That doesn't make sense." And I thought that at first, that to have some sort of profound experience you have to go to a specific place, on a beautiful retreat.
>
> You would go outside and somebody would guide you.

She thought she was going to miss out by not going somewhere, but instead what it did was help her realize how terribly disconnected she was from the place that she lived. A place she realized she knew close to nothing about. She felt attached to her home but didn't have a deeper connection to place until the forest therapy training.

> I thought I was connected to nature. But when I started doing some of these practices about really intentionally slowing down, I realized I was at the tip of the iceberg of my own awareness, and that I had no idea what was below that.

Nicole shared that it was probably one of the most impactful nature experiences she's ever had.

> I'm tearing up a little bit thinking about it because, I think, *What have we lost? What have we been so disconnected from?* It's incredibly sad and I didn't know it was so sad until I started doing this work.
>
> It's profound. As I'm telling this beautiful story about connection, it's also this profound sense of loss. And I think every time I engage in this way, I feel so connected. This is amazing. Wow. And there's so much more I could be connected with.
>
> Research shows that the more connected we are to nature, the more likely we are to take sustainable action. But you can't research somebody into caring. You have to have a personal connection.

Our experiences in nature are an embodied experience. But it is important to find whatever words we can. We seek the words because without the words, we can't share it.

The spirit of reciprocity—the way of our ancestors—is to give in return. It's not a one-way street. When we recognize all of the benefits we receive from nature, the more we are inclined to take environmental action. If we don't feel this way, then it's a good bet that we are not actually very connected to nature.

We need to protect what's giving us so much.

Sometimes we know better yet we are caught unaware. Nature can sneak up on us.

> "We are so often looking at our feet that we miss the broader world around us."
>
> —John Perkins

Nature Speaks to Us

John Perkins spent his childhood summers in the mountains of New Hampshire, in a small cottage that his grandfather had built in the early 1900s. An only child in an area with no other children around, he kept himself entertained in the forest along Mascoma Lake, which is Algonquin for "Big Bear Lake."

Fancying himself King Arthur, he talked to the trees and imagined them to be his Knights of the Round Table. There was Guinevere, Galahad, and Lancelot among the deciduous trees and fir.

Little did John realize that he was practicing shamanic journeying at this young age. He was learning to listen to the spirits of the forest.

Many years later, John was in the Peace Corps, deep in the Amazonian jungle. He became very sick, could not keep any food down, was dying—until he was healed by a shaman and invited to be trained by him. John recalls that much of what he learned was not exactly new to him, but, for the first time, he had a mentor to guide him.

Growing up, he sometimes thought he might be crazy, although his parents never discouraged his active "imagination." He always knew that there was incredible information to be learned from nature, the spirit of the forest.

Although John moved to the other side of the continent, he returns every summer for two months to enjoy the cottage and the forest of his childhood.

A few years ago, he visited his childhood summer home as usual and got into the rhythm of spending early mornings on the lake, writing his current book, and then capping the day off with a run through one of the trails in the woods near his cottage.

One nice, sunny day in early September, John could feel the change in the seasons already.

> There was a distinct smell that I cannot describe. Crows were congregating and the other birds were starting their migration to a warmer climate.

John picked a trail, about two and half miles, that was steep and led up the mountain. This trail was a sensory experience. Part of it was a dry riverbed that had pebbles that he could feel through his thin-soled running shoes. There were also thin branches on either side of the trail; rather than dodge them, he let the leaves massage his body as he passed.

> As usual, I was following my own guidance of not focusing on my feet as I ran. Rather, I would observe the path for several yards ahead of me and then look around, being present with the forest. But this point on the path, with loose pebbles and a

rock ledge, required me to watch my footing. I was temporarily distracted from the nature around me.

John feels that the idea of not focusing on our feet—a technique used today by indigenous people in the Amazon and traditionally by Native North Americans—is symbolic.

> We are so often looking at our feet that we miss the broader world around us. What's the stock market doing today? Who said what in Congress? We forget about the long term, the path ahead. We are caught up in the minutiae.

It's an important philosophical concept. Once, John taught a workshop at the Omega Institute in Rhinebeck, New York that was actually called, "Walk Without Watching Your Feet." And someone, needing to cut back on the copy in the catalog, erroneously edited it down to "Walking Without Feet"!

> So I was on this trail, watching my feet, when suddenly I heard a noise and stopped. A black bear cub dashed across the trail right in front of me and climbed up a tree. Then, moments later, another cub ran in the opposite direction, crossing the trail as well.

His eyes followed this second cub, only to find its mother, a large black bear, perhaps four hundred pounds, looking at him.

> Growing up in New Hampshire, I'd learned that you are never to get between a mother and her cub. In fact, I always thought, *How could anyone be so stupid as to do that?* But now I found myself in exactly this position.

> The mother was standing on her hind legs with one cub on the left side of the trail and the other cub next to John, up in a fir tree. To make matters worse, the cub started crying. "I had never heard this sound before and I couldn't believe how much it sounded like a human baby crying."

John had also learned that, in most cases, you never want to run from a large mammal. In fact, he talks about how to deal with predator encounters in his book *Touching the Jaguar*.

> You don't run from them. If you do, they'll give you chase! I'd heard that the best action is to make yourself appear as large as possible by waving your arms and making loud noises.
>
> But my instincts—perhaps we can say the spirit of the trees, of the forest—told me to kneel down on one knee, to make myself small. I looked up at the baby cub, and with the softest, gentlest voice, I spoke to her. I told her how honored and grateful I felt to be in her presence. Then I turned to her mother and said the same to her.

Rather than feeling fear, John says that he felt awe and gratitude. Although he has spent many years in this wilderness, with abundant sightings of black bears and catamounts (mountain lions that are the equivalent to South American jaguars), he had never come between a mother and its cub before.

After what seemed like hours, the cub finally climbed down and ran across the trail to her momma. John kept still and quiet.

Then he finally, slowly got to his feet and continued up the trail. When he reached the top of the mountain, he was still able to hear them among the brush, cubs talking with their mother.

> For me, it was a great confirmation to listen—truly listen—to the voices of nature. The voices were clearly telling me to be small and humble and respectful. It was a beautiful encounter which I am deeply honored to have had.

Nature speaks to us so strongly. We can see how people are waking up to the fact that we are not apart from nature, but rather a *part* of nature.

Not long after, when John was back in the Amazon rainforest on a shamanic tour, he went down the river with a member of the group in a two-person kayak. It was deep in Achuar territory, requiring a small plane and dugout canoe ride from the end of the road.

As they rounded a bend, they saw a huge jaguar swimming across the river. The river current was pushing them ever closer to her. John had just finished writing his book, *Touching the Jaguar,* and here he was, just about to touch one in waking life!

John paddled backward to keep a distance, as she turned to them. Unperturbed, she continued crossing the river. She climbed up the riverbank, glanced nonchalantly at them, shook off the water, and disappeared into the forest.

Suddenly, a flock of Hoatzin birds—large, striking creatures of the Amazon—burst into the air, nearly colliding with their kayak as they scattered in panic to escape a jaguar.

> Once we returned to the dock, a group of young Achuar men urged me to join them on a large canoe to retrace my steps.
>
> When we reached the riverbank, we got out and found the jaguar tracks. "Touch her tracks," they said to me. "There is magic in them." And so, I did. It was a beautiful confirmation and offered a symbolic ending to my book.

Back to New Hampshire, John's childhood place is this beautiful land where his family has lived since the 1600s. He was told that his great, great, great grandmother was kidnapped by the Abnaki Indians in the 1700s. She was raised by them and actually became a part of their tribe until she was rescued. But she didn't want to return to the white man's ways.

> I guess I have an echo of that experience in my DNA.
>
> The forest where I met the mother bear and her cubs is the forest where the trees, King Arthur and Queen Guinevere, talked to me, taught me to be a part of, rather than apart from, nature. And, you know, the Amazon rainforest is part of that same great body of wisdom.

Nature is an amazing teacher. Even the coronavirus comes from nature. It too is teaching us. Teaching us that we can change, and we must change. We can even enjoy change.

"...to look into their tiny black eyes, and feel a divine presence."

—Maureen Calamia

Squirrel Momma

When my son was little, he told me about a dream he had that he was a baby squirrel and I fed him and took care of him. So sweet!

But it took another fifteen years or so before I became a true baby squirrel caregiver.

In 2006, I heeded a call for volunteers at our local nature center. I had recently been working part-time as a marketing consultant and had time during my week to help out.

As it turned out, my office skills were the best I could offer them.

After several years of office work, I heard about a special class they were offering and decided to sign up with my husband and son. It was a class on care for baby squirrels that are orphaned for one reason or another. Depending on the season (which is late winter and summer), the center is often overwhelmed with squirrels and in need of a few extra volunteers in the wildlife rehabilitation department.

For the past few years, I've been bringing home the babies, feeding them at regular intervals throughout the day, and for the tiniest ones, even during the night.

It is a humbling experience. Sometimes the babies don't make it. But most of the time they do, and then they are finally released back into the wild.

But those precious times when I am feeding them, there is such a tremendous gratitude in having this intimate connection with them. I am their surrogate mommy. They trust me inherently with their care. Until they don't anymore.

When they get bigger, near the release stage, they are wild! I've had a few squirrels lunge at me and bite me. Their sharp nails scratch the heck out of my hands. But they mean no harm to me.

I am so grateful for each opportunity to have this close bond, for a few weeks, to look into their tiny black eyes, and feel a divine presence.

Nature Divination

Nature is full of symbols and metaphors. But our encounters with wildlife connect us with another being that we can relate to more readily than a rock.

Many of us anthropomorphize our relationships with our pets. We ascribe human characteristics, behavior, and emotion to our furry friends.

Essentially, when we reflect on what we perceive to be messages from the natural world, we are practicing nature divination. Years ago, I came across a book that helped me tune into this practice. And it has helped many people, like me. *Animal-Speak: The Spiritual and Magical Powers of Creatures Great & Small*, by Ted Andrews became a bible for my practice.

Whenever I had an odd wildlife encounter, I would turn to this book. In it is wisdom from many ancient and shamanic traditions, in how they would interpret meaning from an experience.

It is not just the animal itself that has meaning, but their behavior and movements as well. We can consider the actions of the animal and the cardinal direction of its path, as well as its direction relative to our location. Numbers also have significance. A lone duck is different than a family of ducks.

These traditions revolve around the behaviors of these animals. How they survive, their strengths and weaknesses, how they mate and procure food, and how they build their habitats. There is much to learn and consider when reflecting on wildlife encounters.

You can consider the information below which is commonly accepted as basic interpretations of these symbols, or use a reference book such as *Animal-Speak*.

Using compass directions:

> **East:** new beginnings, ancestors, family
>
> **South:** illumination, clarity, heart-centered, compassion, masculinity
>
> **West:** completion, creativity, children
>
> **North:** inner journey, imagination, femininity

Analyzing movement in relation to your physical body:

> **Left to right:** from concept/idea stage to action/manifestation stage—ready to launch or step forward
>
> **Right to left:** from action stage back to contemplation stage—need to think things through or step back
>
> **Front to back:** something arriving, coming at you
>
> **Back to front:** something leaving, release

Finally, using numbers in your translation:

> **1:** independence, leadership, uniqueness, possibly arrogance
>
> **2:** partnership, collaboration
>
> **3:** creativity, birth, mystic, sacred
>
> **4:** stability, responsibility, hard work
>
> **5:** change, transformation, occasionally scattered
>
> **6:** service, family, home

7: wisdom, seeking

8: money, power, possibly overbearing or greedy

9: healer, compassion

Invitation: Be Still

As shared by many of these stories, the most important qualities to nurture for interaction with wildlife are stillness and observation. Go outside and sit in a park or your yard and be as still and quiet as you can. Then observe. When we mindlessly enter a landscape, wildlife scatters. But they eventually return to continue whatever they were doing. Try to remain as still as you can and sit for twenty to thirty minutes. It can take some time for the animals to return. Have patience. When you are done, journal about your experience. Who visited? What was their activity and movement in relation to direction and your body?

You can complete this exercise with a question in mind, or just see what arises for you.

Invitation: Keep Track of Unusual Encounters

Keep track of unusual encounters with wildlife. Either 1) an unusual animal that you do not encounter on a regular basis (such as the bison Hobie encountered in the road), or 2) unusual activity by an animal that you regularly encounter (recall Janine Benyus's story of the ducks surrounding her kayak).

Ponder the symbolism of their visit. What do you associate with that animal? What do other cultures believe their meaning represents? Was there something you were just wondering about, a decision that needed to be made when they showed up? What was the animal doing? What direction was it moving? Is there a gut feeling you get when you ponder the meaning? Do any of the thoughts about the meaning feel right to you in your body? Like it just clicks with you? Do you have a sense of the message regarding this encounter? Has anything changed with your perspective of a situation that is currently happening in your life? Journal your experience and insights.

CHAPTER 6

Weather, Cosmos, and Natural Phenomena

"If people looked at the stars each night, they'd live a lot differently."

—Bill Watterson

Weather is one of those encounters with nature that many of us complain about. What's the weather forecast? It's raining again! When will this heat wave be over?

With modern technology, we can now mostly shield ourselves from the worst weather challenges, and yet, we still love to talk about it.

Why? I think it's because we have no control over it. It is one of those aspects of life that we cannot change. It is what it is.

But being able to forecast or predict approaching weather is important. It gives us a sense of some control, or perhaps, preparation.

Views of nature have been associated with an increased sense of well-being, not just because of natural light, but the importance of seeing the sky and anticipating what is coming.

Observing the sky during the day is available to all of us at some point in our lives. But the night sky? Not so much.

I grew up in the 1970s on Long Island, outside of New York City. And due to light pollution, it wasn't until I camped in Maine when I was nineteen years old that I saw the Milky Way for the first time. I was determined to not let that happen to my children, and when they were little, I will never forget sharing the night sky with them in New Hampshire. They were amazed!

When she was just a baby, I would prop my daughter up to see the moon before bedtime. Her first word was "moon." Just last night, she pulled me outside to see the full moon lunar eclipse. She and I stood there in amazement, never losing that sense of awe and wonder.

We have an inherent right to see the heavens. But the stars have been taken from so many of us. And when that happens, we dissociate ourselves from this intimate, yet powerful, connection to the natural world. This chapter looks at our connection with what is above our heads.

> "Because when you put these ideas into words, it somewhat crushes that intimate connection. As if preserving the integrity of a deep, intimate secret."
>
> —Sofia Batalha

We've Lost the Stars

Sofia Batalha was raised by two scientists. Her father was an engineer; her mother, a biologist. Although they remained in Portugal all their lives, as she has, her parents seemingly distanced themselves from the dogma of the entrenched Roman Catholic traditions. The culture was embedded with deference to Christian authority (namely, priests) who served as mediators between us and the sacred. The mysterious nature of the universe was not for us to ponder.

Her parents? You could say they were rebels in their time. They refused to accept the prevailing notions and were captivated by reason. Even her maternal grandfather was a devoted follower of the "science god."

To them, everything in the universe could be named. It could be dissected and reduced down to its parts. Life itself is attributed to mechanical processes. To wonder and contemplate the mysteries of the world was to succumb to the superstitions and folklore of primitive, uneducated people.

Sofia said, "My childhood was robbed of the bedtime stories of witches, goblins, and princesses in fantastical castles. Of talking trees and mice and falling into a rabbit hole, leading to magical lands of cakes, rainbow skies, and never-ending days."

With a gleam in her eye, she says, "But there was once my own magical place."

Her family owned a summer home in Monte Gordo, a sleepy beachside village where fishermen and traditional crafts were abundant.

It was an ancient village built on the outskirts of the dunes. The roads were always filled with sand blown over by the winds. The traditional homes would start at the first story up to keep out the shifting sand. With no roof tiles, they built terraces at the top to dry and preserve olives, almonds, figs, tomatoes, and even fish.

Each house was painted in bright hues of yellow, orange, blue, and pink.

During Sofia's childhood in the 1980s, Portugal still had an abundance of old coastal villages, practically untouched by modern life.

> We stayed there every summer since I was born. Vacation was three months long, so one-quarter of my young life was spent reorganizing my rhythms with the flow of this simple, humble community.
>
> The summer days were so hot, not much happened. But when the sun set, the town would come to life! All the villagers would sit out on their porch or gather in the village square. That was the living room.

> Me and the other children would play on the big expansive beach which extended for twenty kilometers. We knew where to spot the abundance of chameleons that could always be found along the shifting dunes. The forest was living through the gentle and warm afternoon breeze. I would lie on the ground, watching the clouds and trees play in the sun and shade.
>
> This magical place had so much to offer a child of wonder, but one spot stands out above all others.
>
> The beach at night. The sand and the surf encompassed my senses. The hot, gentle breeze was like a smooth surface washing over my skinny, bare arms and legs. It was a warm embrace from nature herself.

As a child, she would lie on the soft, sweet-smelling sand, tinged with the scent of the white flowers that grew in the dunes. She watched the night sky above. We would cry out in excitement when we saw a shooting star...all the others would be envious, until they saw one.

> I wondered at this massive cloud of stars that I later learned was named the Milky Way. I could see why it was called that. The clouds of light looked like puddles of milk after I had spilled my cup (which happened way too often).

Every August, she looked forward to Perseid's meteor shower, which happened like clockwork. *Why,* she would wonder, *does that happen every summer?*

> When I was six years old, I would go with my father down to the beach at night.

Her father was born to a poor cow-herding family in the hills, but fled to Lisbon at the age of sixteen to study and find his own way. He was very proud of his accomplishments and intelligence. There was no shortage of answers from Sofia's father.

> So, when I asked him about the mysteries of the night sky, his response was a mathematical lesson of distance and light years—information that no child would understand. My six-year-old self didn't hear any of that. She wanted no part of a mechanistic explanation. Completely engulfed in the magic of that moment by the ocean, holding my father's hand, I stared up with wonder.

In this sacred place, she found the antidote to her family discourse, somewhere she could disappear into the limitless curiosity of nature.

When she was in her teens, she had a habit of sneaking out to the beach at night. Sometimes with friends, sometimes alone, to capture that magic again.

> Did I talk about the expanse and the mystery unfolding before us? Very rarely. Because when you put these ideas into words, it somewhat crushes that intimate connection. As if preserving the integrity of a deep, intimate secret.

When she turned seventeen, her parents sold the home after increasing pressure from realtors hoping to develop the area for tourism. The wide beaches, gentle currents, and Mediterranean climate made it ideal to attract northern Europeans.

Scores of families moved away from the ancestral lands. In the excitement to modernize, many moved to big cities.

Just like those villages, as time passed, Sofia did disconnect with this other self, but somehow it stayed deep inside, dormant.

Although in college she studied the arts, graphic design, and earned post-graduate degrees in museum organization and communications, her mindset was really driven by linear thinking, grounded in the material world.

Even after college, Sofia started her own small design company. She was successful in the material sense and was able to express her creativity.

> Then suddenly, the fountain inside me dried up. I wasn't able to return to Monte Gordo for years, having grieved not only my personal loss, but those of the villagers, their traditional ways, and the earth itself.

But after the birth of her first child at the age of thirty-three, she somehow found the courage to visit for a few hours.

> It was heartbreaking. Unbearable to witness the loss of the charming, traditional houses, the villagers, their way of life—all gone. Replaced by skyscrapers, by hotels and condominiums, all catering to tourists.
>
> The villagers that stayed were either working in tourism or didn't work at all. Fishing was forbidden in the bay to make it safer for tourists.
>
> For all the deep hurt that visit inflicted, I see that it was a necessary step to heal and move on. It gave me the ground to embrace mystery and be who I am today. I recognized that I was, as a child, able to embrace who I was, not who my family expected me to be. It gave me assurance that there is something unknowable there. Something that is alive. Something more that doesn't need to be explained or measured to be real.

And there was one such event that seemed unreal. Sofia and her husband camped in the desert in Jordan. On the morning of New Year's Day, she rose before sunrise and stepped out of the tent, without any particular intention or objective.

> The coldness of the desert at night is sometimes a shock, but I started walking along the rocky stone pillars in the sand, the soft sound of my footsteps cradled by the giving earth. *The magic of the silence*, I thought.

She found herself perched on a large rock, mesmerized by the vastness of the night sky, as she did on that magical beach long ago. The light of the sun was just starting to creep over the horizon.

> While in my reverie, I was startled by a big whooshing sound that drew my attention upward to a large black bird, flapping its expansive wings over my head. Suddenly, that fountain of sacred connection, of mystery and magic, started pouring forth again.

This experience gave her the impetus to return to that inner child, the true authentic self, that her early experiences nurtured.

> I felt able to fully step into my power as a spiritual woman. My experiences in Monte Gordo ignited what I needed to alchemize outside of the rational mind. This was the place and space I required to reconnect to the experience of just being. It connected what was severed before, allowing the nature within me to open up and grow as it never had before.
>
> I am so grateful for the luminous night sky and the sand that supports it. I have bottles of sand from both of these places, which remind me every day who I am and what I need to do.

I interviewed Sofia recently for my podcast and we discussed Monte Gordo and her childhood wonders there. Sometimes new information arises when we have space to reflect. And Sofia's words sent shivers down my spine.

She said, "We've lost the stars. That beach in Monte Gordo is no longer there. So many of these places are no longer."

Sofia is right. Light pollution is increasingly encroaching on our dark skies.

According to research estimates, one-third of humanity cannot see the Milky Way, including nearly 80 percent of the population in North America! The future impact of this on our collective sense of wonder, as well as the recognition of our place in this universe, is incomprehensible.

> "The planets, just like all of creation, are there to help us through our journey of life here."
>
> —Amanda Walsh

Mythology of the Stars

While writing this book, I was drawn to contact Amanda "Pua" Walsh, founder and CEO of a popular online astrology community, to interview. I thought it would be interesting to learn of her stories around nature connection. And it certainly was.

Amanda opened our interview with this statement:

> We can go into active communion and relationship with these planetary beings. We can draw upon our resonance to their energy when we need it. I believe they enjoy it, too.

Her big *aha* moment took place several years ago on her lanai in Maui. She was enjoying the beautiful nature around her. Ocean waves crashing on the beach, trees swirling in the wind, birds enjoying the last bit of sunlight, getting ready for the night. And then, the sun set.

Instead of going back into the house, as she always did after sunset, this evening she sat there for a while. The sky got darker, and eventually the planets and stars came out.

> For the first time, I got it. That there is no difference between these planetary beings and trees! It's all nature. It was a dawn of awareness for me. We are just as connected to the planets as we are the birds and flowers. We have an opportunity to enter into communion with them and hear them.
>
> There are an untold number of cycles happening in the sky at any given time. A great celestial clock. The movement of the planets and stars swirl and spiral in a kaleidoscope of energy. And from an astrological perspective, we realize that we are in

a co-creative process with these energies that manifest as events and experiences in our lives.

We can all do this—have a deep connection with the planets. It's hard to describe how communication happens but we have to know that the archetype of each of the planets are within us. For example, when we need warrior energy, we can call on Mars, the warrior planet.

But this communication didn't come naturally for Amanda. At first, Amanda approached relationship with nature as more of a skeptic. She needed to experience it firsthand.

It happened in 2020, when Amanda decided to experiment with planetary communication to help her with a challenging situation involving her eleven-year-old daughter.

> My daughter doesn't like change. She had been at the Waldorf School for most of her childhood and was embraced as part of the family there. But she needed to move schools and I knew this would be a huge upheaval in her life. She started to have meltdowns leading up to the first day at her new school.

So, the night before her first day at the new school, Amanda was inspired to share the story of Inanna with her daughter. According to folklore, Inanna is the goddess queen of the heavens, also known as Venus.

As the Mesopotamian myth goes, Inanna ventured into the underworld to meet her demons. At each of the seven gates she passed through, she had to remove an article or accessory of clothing, until she was naked and pure. When there, Inanna met her sister, who then killed her. Inanna went on to emerge from the underworld, transformed, and take her rightful place on the throne in heaven, as the planet Venus.

The story tracks the literal pathway of Venus in the sky.

Amanda told her daughter this myth about the challenges of transformation and change to teach her an important lesson. When we meet our demons head on, and go through the fires of transformation, we are able to emerge totally new.

Her daughter was enthralled. Amanda told her, "In some ways, this is your initiation. Demons are telling you that you cannot meet this challenge. This is your opportunity to emerge from this experience more glorious than ever. But you have to say yes and step up to it."

The next morning, before waking her daughter up, Amanda looked out the kitchen window and saw Venus, the morning star, outside. *How beautiful and appropriate for this big day*, she thought.

Then, she went into her daughter's room and turned on soft, ceremonial music.

Madeline awoke and Amanda said to her, "You won't believe this, but look out the window."

Her daughter cried, "Venus!"

The rest of that morning went smoothly as they prepared for the first day of school. Madeline was more calm and composed than ever. Amanda could not believe how well it went.

At the end of the school day, on the car ride home, Madeline said that she really loved her new school.

Amanda turned to her and asked, "You were so calm this morning. How did that happen?"

Madeline answered, "You showed me Venus."

This transformative experience with her daughter and the message of Venus taught Amanda that true connection is not only possible, but probable.

> The planets, just like all of creation, are there to help us through our journey of life here. Just engaging in respectful collaboration is all we need to feel their presence and guidance.

✦ ✯ ✦

> "That sunrise was the most glorious and illuminating
> of my entire life."
>
> —Betsy Perluss

The Lunar Light

When I asked Betsy Perluss, PhD, about a profound nature experience, she replied that yes, she has had so many. But they can be considered very ordinary experiences, too.

She holds space for that paradox for many people participating in the nature retreats that she leads as part of the School of Lost Borders in California.

Betsy has done her own "vision fast," a four-day solo retreat in the desert, about twenty times.

> Sleeping alone under the stars in the desert. It is profoundly ordinary, ordinarily profound. No retreat is the same as the one before. What shows up is what I need at that moment in my life.

About ten years ago, Betsy went out alone for a solo fast. At the time, she had just received tenure at California State University. She found it to be a rather grueling process of creating a "brag sheet" documenting her achievements, including articles published, presentations given, student testimonials, volunteerism. She jumped through many massive hoops to achieve it.

> It was such a masculine-oriented process that it drained my psyche. I felt so disconnected from my body, instincts, and feelings. I longed to cultivate my deeper feminine qualities, which had been pushed to the side for months.

During the final night of these fasts it is always recommended to do an all-night vigil. But, since she had done this so many times, she thought to herself, *There's no way I'm going to do that tonight. I'm beyond that.* So, she stayed in her tent.

Then, at about eleven o'clock, the full moon woke her. It was so bright and intense. The light was shining into her face saying, "wake up!"

Betsy argued with the moon. No, she was going to stay warm in her sleeping bag. But the moon kept insisting she get up.

Until finally, she got up into the freezing cold night. And she started walking.

She decided to walk to a circle of huge boulders. It was on an old migration path in the back country of Death Valley, which led to a spring.

> Somehow, I got lost! What should have been a thirty-minute walk turned into an all-night vigil. I was so disoriented that I didn't know where I was in the valley. I had been here so many times that I wasn't panicked. But I needed to walk slowly and to follow my intuition.

With the light of the moon, Betsy resigned herself to trusting that lunar consciousness within her. The fact that she walked all night didn't make sense. She should have found her way back more quickly. Yet there was an incredible feeling of being grounded with her feet on the sand in the wash. Seeing the outline of plants and stones. She was guided by an inner lunar quality, derived from the sky.

> I got the deep sense that the moon was illuminated by the sun, somewhere out there. It occurs to me more now as I reflect on this experience. That solar consciousness, the masculine, can be so oppressive on its own, when it's a one-sided patriarchal consciousness. But when the moon is being illuminated, it can be a supportive sun, not oppressive.
>
> The sun illuminates the moon. It doesn't dominate the moon.

Around six o'clock or so, the sky started to turn a bit pink. The sun was rising, and she was amazed that she did, against her plan, walk all night.

> That sunrise was the most glorious and illuminating of my entire life.
>
> In the moonlight I could see the outline of things, but now, with the sun, I could start to see everything around me take form, color, and shape. Finally, I could see where I was. I could find myself.

This experience gave Betsy the capacity to walk in her lunar consciousness, not along the path that was rational to follow.

As a result, about two years later, Betsy left her position at the university, for better or worse. She realized that this position would eventually drain her psychic energy.

Suddenly, she found herself in a lunar landscape and has been there ever since.

> It has been challenging. At the university, I had an identity, a schedule, I knew exactly what was expected of me and had a direct path to follow. Then I realized—who am I? Where do I show up? It has been confusing, but now, years later, it feels familiar and nourishing. It feels like where I belong.

Even though she feels lost at times, she has a relationship with the moon and with her own psyche that she can trust.

> Lunar consciousness is so different. It's not about doing the work of external approval or acquiring a name or status. It's from the heart. Because you love it.
>
> The heart is essential to cultivate true lunar consciousness. The moon shines because it loves to illuminate. It doesn't want to force or dominate.
>
> It is about following my nature, not because I need to achieve success. Why does a flower blossom in its own unique way? Not because it's trying to impress the garden-tender; it's just what it does.

Weather is something that is a constant in our everyday lives. We check the weather report before we step out of the house. We anticipate the forecast for the upcoming weekend. So much of our lives are impacted by this natural phenomenon. But sometimes, our encounters with weather can be life or death.

> "...getting into a storm at night in these conditions, well, that's scary."
>
> —Oliver Heath

Finding Oneself in Nature

Oliver Heath grew up in Brighton, a town on the southern coast of England known for attracting holiday crowds with its fresh air, expansive beaches, and seafront views. It was an idyllic childhood. His days were spent playing and swimming in the sea, building forts, climbing trees. Like many children at the time, he was given freedom to explore, off with his friends until the dinner bell rang.

> When I read Richard Louv's book *The Last Child in the Woods*, I thought that was my childhood. We were given the opportunity to roam.

Oliver was always looking for adventure. He was scuba diving at age fourteen and a windsurfing instructor at eighteen when he went to study architecture at University College London. "Although I was interested in the design of buildings, my nature-based experiences in childhood gave me a strong desire to somehow fuse nature and architecture."

In Brighton, the Royal Pavilion, a fantastical palace inspired by Indo-Chinese styles, fascinated Oliver as a child.

Near the palace are two beautiful piers that go out into the sea. His earliest memories include walking along these structures, seeing the waves roll beneath the slats of wood. He grew up in a place that was very much about connecting to nature for well-being. It's very different from a big city like London, or an industrial town.

After graduating from architecture school, Oliver had a thirst for adventure. He joined a small crew to sail a yacht from Portsmouth, England, to a port in the Mediterranean. It was a small, thirty-foot yacht with just three other crew members, each an interesting character in their own right.

The captain, as it turned out, was an alcoholic, while his son was described as an "aggressive and dangerous young man." The third crew member was a retired headmaster. Despite Oliver's better instincts, he sailed off with them across the English Channel. When they reached the Bay of Biscay, known for its deep water and dangerous storms, they ran into some weather.

After an exciting day of sailing, the winds picked up, creating dynamic waves. They were flying along at a great clip as the sun was setting. Oliver looked out across the water and saw a dead shark. A bad omen for their small yacht?

> Looking to the west, I saw big storm clouds on the horizon. And getting into a storm at night in these conditions, well, that's scary.

As the storm approached, they were putting down sails when the captain was struck in the head by a spinnaker pole. Bleeding, he went below deck to patch himself up, and proceeded to get drunk.

The winds continued to pick up, and then they found themselves enveloped in mist. The mist was so dense, he could barely see the waves that were crashing over the boat. They had to tether themselves to the cabin of the yacht so as not to fall overboard. Even though they reduced the sails, they were still crashing around.

> Then suddenly, there was this enormous tanker that appeared out of the mist. They hadn't seen us. Our captain, in his drunken stupor, hadn't put the radar reflector up, so the ship didn't even know we were there. I just remember looking straight up—it was that close. I thought, *This ship is going to smash us to pieces*. But somehow it just missed us.

Oliver was trying to look after the captain, who was so drunk at this point he was rolling around the bow of the boat. As Oliver leaned forward to grab him, the main sail swung over his head and the main sheet rope struck him in the forehead. It almost knocked him out. He was stumbling around the boat, delirious, blood pouring out of his head.

> I had to be taken down below to get patched up and the rest of the crew called a mayday signal. I couldn't quite picture how I'd be airlifted from this boat by a helicopter in the storm.

Their signal wasn't picked up by the coast guard, so they simply had to patch Oliver's head up and continue to sail through the storm. In the morning, they finally reached a little fishing village and the local medical staff stitched him up.

> I recognized the fragility of life and one's ability to put themselves in dangerous situations—specifically, myself. The pursuit of adventure could come at a high price.
>
> It was a very dramatic experience. It clearly left a mental—and I guess also a physical—line in my mind about our fragility on Earth, and how we need to respect nature and understand our boundaries. We are at its mercy. It was a fundamental life lesson. We are not killing the planet; we are killing its habitable biosphere. And without that, we cannot live here.

When Oliver reflects on these times when he was craving adventure, he realizes now that he was craving something deeper.

> I was finding myself. I guess it was my naïveté that sometimes resulted in dangerous situations. Near-death experiences. Sometimes magical, sometimes downright scary. The line between the two is often quite narrow.

Since studying architecture, Oliver has become a human-centered designer who believes that experiences in and of nature should be inherent in our lives.

> As a young architect, I recognized that I was happiest when surrounded by nature, so I did my best to fuse these two concepts, to create buildings that would somehow support that connection. But traditionally, nature and architecture are at odds. We design spaces to keep nature out.

About twelve years ago, Oliver discovered biophilic design, a new emerging discipline, which incorporates nature into the built environment. People in these spaces can have a more symbiotic relationship with nature.

Now, Oliver is a top biophilic design advocate, helping others understand and harness their connections to nature to benefit both people and planet.

> Most of us have had profound moments in our lives that were deeply rooted in nature. These are multisensory experiences, unlike those that we typically experience in the safety and security of a building. But these experiences don't happen that often. By contrast, we also need to cultivate lots of little moments in nature. We can address that by experiencing nature in the buildings that are most important in our lives: our homes, schools, hospitals, and workspaces.
>
> Yes, we can experience nature on our summer holiday, but we also need to connect often—daily, in fact—to the natural world around us. Noticing a beautiful sunset, frost on the grass, a murmuration of birds flying across the sky. These moments

allow us to have a more intimate connection with the spaces, places, and people in our lives.

So, what did Oliver do during lockdown? Well, in addition to all the little nature moments he talked about, he also got his license to sail his own yacht. Hopefully, he'll have better weather—and crewmates—next time!

We are taught from an early age that we are separate from the natural world. So, naturally, that extends to weather patterns. But what if we can work or co-create with these patterns of energy that swirl around our planet? Is that possible? This next contributor shares an experience of doing just that.

> "There was silence. Everyone was shocked."
>
> —Sandra Ingerman

Co-Creating with Conscious Intention and Magic

Communication with nature can occur unknowingly or with intention, purpose, and a mission. Some of us have greater capacity than most to manifest this sort of magic, but it is clear to me that we all have it lying dormant within.

Then there is Sandra Ingerman, a renowned shaman for the last forty years. She teaches all over the world and her specialty is teaching shamanic healing and ceremonial work.

> Ceremonies are a sacred act that help people find a sense of stability and center. They step out of their humanness and

> into their own divinity. Ceremony is the most powerful way to do this.

It's no coincidence that Sandra shared her experience with two powerful ceremonies and how nature speaks through them.

> I have always looked to lead my retreats in places of nature, when possible, to allow participants the ability to wander in nature. Also, my ceremonies—namely the fire ceremony—are best performed at a firepit, although it can be done in an indoor fireplace. Not all retreat centers allow burning fires outdoors as there can be obvious fire danger.

And like so many retreat leaders, Sandra has had to work with the elements.

> For each retreat, I would always have some fear that the weather wouldn't cooperate. That we'd get rained out. I really didn't want my students to miss the opportunity for an outdoor ceremony. So, the first thing I'd do when I arrived at each center would be to visit the firepit and talk to the spirits of the land, the helping and compassionate ancestors, the spirit of Fire, and the helpful spirits. I would give offerings of tobacco and blue corn. Essentially, I would ask for their support.

This offering ritual was something she developed throughout her years teaching.

> I was self-taught in shamanism, so no one told me about the compassionate ancestors that live on the land, but it was something that I just intuitively felt could help. And believe me, I had all types of weather events occur during my training retreats, but I never once had to cancel a ceremony. At one event, the winds were really high during the day... The fire department refused to allow the ceremony. But fifteen minutes before the ceremony would have begun, the wind stopped. It

> was in the desert and was extremely unlikely for the winds to stop, but they did.

Is it a coincidence? Or something more?

"I believe that if we work cooperatively and show honor, respect, and kindness toward the land and all of life, we will be supported," she said.

In 1995, Sandra was holding a soul retrieval workshop in a church in Tennessee.

> I told them, we're going to do some drumming and meditative work. I didn't mention soul retrieval, as they might not agree to hosting us. But that night, a crazy synchronicity occurred when they served us stuffed sole for dinner after the group had performed soul retrievals on each other, bringing back parts of the soul that were lost through trauma.

This workshop took place during Hurricane Opal, originally a Category 4 storm that dumped three to five inches of rain on the state.

The night of the fire ceremony, the storm was wild. There was a room with a tiny fireplace, and Sandra figured that she could make it work. But the group of about forty people would have been packed like sardines.

She checked in with the firekeepers—a few people designated to tend the fire—and they had just begun building it when Sandra entered the room to see how things were going. No one was particularly impressed with the ambience, but in ceremony, it's the intention that matters more than the setting or appearance. As the group began to gather, they noticed something remarkable: the rain and wind had magically stopped.

> There was silence. Everyone was shocked. I yelled to all the participants, "Grab a piece of wood and run outside!" We all ran with our drums and rattles and whatever wood we could carry. I did my opening invocation with my rattles.

In her workshops, each participant spends the day crafting a talisman that symbolizes an old wound preventing them from fully embracing a life of passion and creativity. At the end, they release the talisman into the fire, letting go of what holds them back.

> The way I do this is everyone works one by one, taking turns only when their heart feels called. They sing and dance next to the fire while releasing their talisman. This process can be very long. Each person dances about what they are letting go of and communes honorably with the fire about being released from the energy blocking them in life.

She typically has about fifty to seventy-five people! As you can imagine, this is not a quick process.

"When the last person returned to the circle that night, I quickly did my closing, thanking the helpful spirits for witnessing and supporting our work," she said. "Immediately after this closing, Opal returned! We were in the eye of the storm, figuratively and literally! I never get tired of these miraculous things. We don't even realize how much support we have."

With the pandemic, Sandra has had to shift all her teaching online, and is teaching mostly about connecting to nature.

> It's amazing what people experience in my classes. We must understand that, although we love hugging trees, we shouldn't just hug a tree. We should stop and ask permission. We can begin our communication with the tree by emanating love and light into it. Then we can start to create a friendship by learning about their life and sharing about ours.

One of the biggest parts of her work is helping people connect with the land they live on.

> Once they do, they experience miracles. People that have been living in their houses for twenty years suddenly see nature reaching out to them. It's not just me having miraculous experiences. People are seeing more animals and birds showing

up as they learn to work in cooperation with the spirits of the land...the helpful, compassionate ancestors.

She teaches people to not only connect through love and light, but start a dialogue.

Ask about its family, its history, what it's seen here. Then start talking about yourself. Treat nature as a friend. Nurture that relationship! Even if you live in a city, it is easy to do this. One can sit on the cement and speak to the spirits of the land and ask the land to tell a story of its history and all it has witnessed. Or you could find a park where you can connect with nature.

We are nature, not part of it. When we open our hearts and show honor, kindness, and respect to the spirits, nature responds to us. Nature gives us what we need. We are part of nature's destiny, as we came here to be caretakers of the earth. We can live in beautiful cooperation together.

I have a strong connection with storms. One particular thunderstorm is still my most powerful nature story from childhood. You'll read about it in Chapter 8. But the one that I share below is a multi-layered experience, full of synchronistic connections.

> "Two minutes later, our front doorbell rang."
>
> —Maureen Calamia

Wild Gaia and the Storm

After visiting the Neolithic site of Newgrange while on a family holiday in Ireland in 2018, I decided to create a stone cairn in our garden. Living on Long Island, which is basically a long, wide barrier beach for the continent, I craved my own mini-mountain or sacred space.

We placed our stone cairn with care near the front garden in the corner of our home. It was placed in the "Helpful People" area of our land, according to feng shui. A structure like this can nurture helpful people in our lives.

About a year later, in August 2020, we had a tropical storm blow through Long Island. I remember sitting at the kitchen table with the natural light and expansive views of the junipers, hollies, and seventy-foot oaks surrounding our home. Although I'm usually very aware of approaching storms, somehow this one escaped my attention until I finally noticed huge wind gusts. I think this storm was stronger than anyone expected it to be.

I was on Zoom with a colleague and the wind seemed to get stronger with each passing moment. I saw some branches fall, and a large one was carried down the street by a strong gust. As I watched the branch pass, one of our large oaks came crashing down across the driveway, onto our front lawn, just missing our cars.

Stunned, I jumped up and closed my meeting. I screamed when I saw the tree fall and felt rather hysterical. My heart was pounding with adrenaline. We ran outside to see the tree lying across our front lawn, branches tangled with a small dogwood and metal from the gutters. Yet, amazingly, there was little damage—again.

Two minutes later, our front doorbell rang. Who could be at our door in the middle of this dangerous storm?

It was a UPS delivery woman, handing me a package.

I said to her, "Why are you out in this storm? Our tree just fell!"

She said, yes, she saw that happen when she pulled up to the house. I guess I wasn't the only one caught off-guard by the weather that day.

I recognized the package, as it was a shipment I was expecting from Spain. It was original artwork called "Gaia." The dramatic timing couldn't have been more significant.

Her appearance (the art), not only that day, but at the exact time it was delivered, certainly made me more respectful of the power of her wrath. She hangs in my home office, across from my desk, as a constant reminder of her strength.

As I said, that downed tree thankfully caused little damage. A few feet farther to the right and it would have landed on our roof, right over the master bedroom! But it took me a few months to realize that we were protected. Weeks later, my husband pointed out the location of the stone cairn we built. The tree fell exactly to the left of the mound, as if directed by guiding hands.

Invitation: Night Sky

On a clear night, go to a place with the least light pollution you can. For many of us, that may be when we're on vacation, away from the city and suburban lights. Lie out on a blanket or recline in a comfortable chair. Spend some time acclimating your eyes. It's great to do this during a meteor shower, if you can time it just right. You can download a phone app to help identify the planets and constellations. There are many free apps available that are easy to use.

But also, be sure to have time to just wonder. See what arises for you.

Invitation: Experience the Weather

If you don't usually take a walk in the rain or wind, why not try it? Dress appropriately so you are as comfortable and dry as possible, and hike into the woods or the beach. Notice the difference in experience from a dry day. What wildlife is visible? What are they doing? What sounds do you hear? Rain on the leaves, wind in the branches? Did you observe anything unusual? Is there a metaphor for what you experienced that can be applied to something that has been bothering you or a decision you need to make? After your walk, journal about the experience.

CHAPTER 7

Synchronistic Life Path Nudges

"To forget how to dig the earth and tend the soil is to forget ourselves."

—**Mahatma Gandhi**

Tending to the earth serves as a metaphor for nurturing our authentic path. Many spiritually minded people feel deeply connected to their purpose and meaning. Yet, how many of us need a gentle nudge to remember—or be reminded—when we stray from that path further down the road?

Synchronicity is a term coined by the Swiss psychologist C.G. Jung to represent meaningful coincidences. Jung believed that events can carry symbolic meaning, much like dreams do. Synchronicities can provide us with deeper understanding of our "encounters" in nature. When reflected upon, they can communicate important messages and offer guidance on relationships or situations in our lives.

Most, if not all, people experience synchronicities, but many dismiss them as happenstance. They may arise as curiosities, such as déjà vu, or repeating numbers, or an obscure topic that keeps popping up into their awareness. Synchronicities can happen when we are in nature. In my own life, I have viewed these as messages with meaning to be explored.

Sometimes I simply see them as a wink and a nod from the universe that I'm on the right path.

In the stories shared in this chapter, all of the participants were either focused on their life's purpose and given additional information, or completely startled by a message that transformed their lives. I loved hearing these stories and I hope they will inspire you as well.

> "Nature sends us messages in the form of symbols and signs all the time. We just have to be present to catch it."
>
> —Craig Chalquist

Nature Is Looking at You, Too

Some years ago, when Dr. Craig Chalquist was a full-time professor at the California Institute of Integral Studies (CIIS) in the San Francisco Bay Area, he was invited to teach a course at Schumacher College in England. It was to be cotaught with a geology professor, Stephen Harding. Harding would teach about the geology of the land and Craig would share about his extensive work on terrapsychology.

> Terrapsychology is a study on how terrain, place, elements, and natural process show up in human psychology, endeavors, and stories, including myth and legend.

Craig was keen to work with Stephen, as he had worked with James Lovelock as a graduate student on his Gaia Theory, which is frequently described as viewing the earth as a single organism. The school is near Devon in the Dartmoor area of England, which is known to have a particularly haunting vibe. *The Hound of the Baskervilles* (a crime novel with several screen adaptations) was set here. And wintertime didn't disappoint. Cold, damp, gloomy days with haunting winds. There were vast stretches of brush in a treeless landscape, and rolling hills punctuated by granite outcroppings.

Since this class was about nature and personal relationship to the land, they dedicated an entire day outside to experiencing nature, despite the formidable weather. They layered up, donned hiking boots, and braved the elements. There was no sound except for the howling of the wind as it traversed the landscape. It was clear that the sound was due to the wind interacting with the abundance of tall grasses and large stones. It added a powerful backdrop to the day, perfect for a Sherlock Holmes mystery.

As the sun cast long shadows on the grasses, the group gathered in a circle. A dozen or so students and the two professors stood a few feet apart over a large circular outcropping of granite. Stephen shared the significance of the geology of these ancient stones, how there was once a sea here with coral reefs and sediments. Over millions of years, with the earth's cycles of heat and pressure, metamorphic and igneous rocks formed. The most outstanding rock is a huge intrusion of granite which covers most of southwest England and peers out of the ground all over this landscape.

Craig prompted the students to imagine that they were looking at this land and could perceive a deeper connection. When suddenly, the notion came to him that, yes, we are all looking at this place, but at the same time, the place is looking at us!

With that shared to the group, unexpectedly, a large black raven flew directly above their heads.

Craig said, "It circled our group once, cawed, and flew off."

They stood there, immobile and silent, coming to grips with the profound confirmation of the message they had received. When we observe and perceive the landscape, the land is doing the same. This active reciprocal relationship was confirmed by the majestic bird, as so often happens when we hear truth.

> At that moment, I realized that the circle we created was mimicking the circle nature created in this field. A circle

of granite. We had arranged ourselves around it in a sort of communion with it.

The raven punctuated this moment, just like the granite surfacing in the soil.

We all, at once, saw this as a gesture, a communication from spirit itself. Nature talking to us symbolically.

He told me that Jung called this synchronicity, but actually this archetypical idea is pervasive in cultures throughout the world.

Nature sends us messages in the form of symbols and signs all the time. We just have to be present to catch it.

Earlier in the program, a few participants had been skeptical about Craig's mythology teachings.

Some students suggested that, when we connect to myth or synchronicity, perhaps we are projecting our desires on experience. But it was clear that after this experience, everyone was blown away.

It was nearly impossible not to see the connection between what transpired. The students could no longer hold onto that worldview.

This story sticks out to me not just for this actual experience, but because of synchronicities in my life. I've had several encounters with crows that were followed by transformative messages. In mythology, crows and ravens are thought of as tricksters, but they are also messengers. Odin, a Norse shaman god, had two ravens as companions. These birds, named Thought and Memory, would fly around the Earth by day, and return nightly to whisper in Odin's ears tales of what they had seen.

This story changed my thinking about synchronicities in a profound way. And it gave me a sense of how science and deep psychology can work together and not be opposed, as long as we approach new ideas with curiosity and an open heart.

Sometimes these happenings occur when we are on our life path, and sometimes when we are completely lost and struggling to find meaning and purpose. The next story is one of the latter experiences, during a really dark time in the participant's life. And one word that changed it all.

"At that moment, I realized this is what I'm called to do."

—Lisa Kahn

The Whisper

Lisa Kahn was taking her two dogs for their daily walk around the lake behind her house. It was early summer in Florida and she had gotten in the habit of rising before the sun, while it was cool and dark. She shares, "There is something about being outside at this time of day which is like no other."

With the vastness of the stars overhead, she felt part of something much greater than her current life situation.

It was 2011 and her life had become "unrecognizable." While Lisa was in the throes of some hideous divorce proceedings, she was having unexpected problems in her business. She had lost a big project and an employee had just quit. On top of all this, most tragically, her teenage daughter suddenly started having grand mal seizures. Every area of her life felt dysfunctional.

> I was unhappy, feeling victimized by life and helpless in these challenges I was facing. I was at the lowest ebb of my life—a dark night of the soul.
>
> I could not seem to escape these burning questions inside myself... *How do I get away from all of this? What should I do to feel better?*

On the morning in question, her two English Springer Spaniels pulled her along the path while she was deep in her grieving thoughts. But as she turned a corner, getting ready to go over the last bridge, she caught a glimpse out of the side of her eye. The sun was peeking over the horizon on the other side of the lake, and the sky lit up in shades of pink and orange before her. She stopped in her tracks.

> Suddenly a strong breeze blew across the lake and lifted my hair up and away from my ears. Then, I heard the word "sanctuary" as if someone had whispered it in my ear.

Everything shifted in that moment.

> I not only heard the word, but I could see it in front of me.

Nothing at all had changed in my world at that moment, but at the same time, *everything had changed*. My body could sense that word at its most comforting and nurturing. A safe place to be, free of suffering.

Her attention then turned to her daughter. She thought, *I need a sanctuary to cope with all of this, but Chloe needs a sanctuary space, too! A place that she can process all that she is going through.*

> At that moment, I realized this is what I'm called to do. So, I took some time to unpack what "sanctuary" means to me, to think more about what that could mean in my work. As an interior designer, I realized that this is what I do for my clients, but had never thought to frame it that way.

Not long after, Lisa traveled for an intensive with her business coach to explore how to integrate this into her business. And when she landed, back from Denver, Lisa had messages from the attorney and her ex-husband that her daughter was in the hospital.

> It really came home to me that I needed to live this idea of sanctuary myself first. That was the message here.

My thinking around all these situations in my life radically shifted. Instead of obstacles, I saw them as a way forward. To see what each experience is teaching me and helping me grow. And sanctuary space can help me process what is happening. To embrace rather than resist.

Writing, blogging, paths to self-exploration. Personal growth, professional growth.

Universal truth. I realized that I was to serve as a channel for it to come forward.

After so much pain and anguish, I'm still on the path of discovering, from a philosophical as well as practical perspective, why the word "sanctuary" appeared to me. It is sublime.

Sometimes we experience words—whispers—of what we are to do. Other times, nature speaks to us in more metaphorical ways. This next story is about the discovery of deeper levels of awakening and one's calling.

> "I was receiving my own confirmation from Nature.
> And this magic has continued."
>
> —Julia Plevin Oliansky

Marked Trees

It was a mild spring day in 2015 when Julia Plevin was taking her usual run in the Sutro Forest, filled with eucalyptus trees, right in the middle of San Francisco. She had just returned from New York, where she had received her master's degree. Suddenly, someone stopped her and asked why there was flagging tape on many of the trees in the park.

Julia hadn't even been aware of the tape as she was lost in her thoughts. So, she shrugged her shoulders and continued her run. But by the time she got back to her apartment, her curiosity and concern for those trees caused her to search online for news about that forest.

> It was as if the trees were flagging me down to pay attention. I was running amidst these beautiful trees, but I wasn't even noticing them.

Julia found out that the eucalyptus forest was planted over a hundred years ago, so the trees were all around the same age and they were wrapped with ivy.

> I couldn't help but fear that this forest would be razed for new development, being right in the heart of the city. I never found out why they were taped, but I assumed they were marking certain trees for removal or ones that required extra care.

Julia's MFA thesis was on the mental health effects of nature. She designed concepts for a nature club in New York City, and then decided to start The Forest Bathing Club when she moved back to San Francisco.

At first, she would take a few friends out to join her, but eventually, she started a Meetup group, and it grew from there.

Through guiding others, Julia developed her own practice of connection. Although many of her participants were at first skeptical—financial investors and tech people—she found that most of them had an experience that altered them in some way. Their personal stories of insight kept her going.

> Forest bathing is a practice of slowing down and listening. It has been a way for me to heal from decades of Lyme Disease. Eventually, I realized that it was not only managing my stress and anxiety, but served as a wonderful way to connect with nature in a spiritual sense.

At this time in her life, she had a good job, but it wasn't fulfilling. "I would go on walks with questions on my mind. Should I quit my job? How will I make money to survive? And I kept hearing 'This path will open up for you. Keep trusting, keep going.' "

And the trees were right. A reporter for a local magazine went on one of her walks and wrote an article on Julia and forest bathing. After that, Julia started to write articles online, and then, as if by magic, a publisher called and asked her to write a book on the topic, which was published in 2019 (*The Healing Magic of Forest Bathing*, Ten Speed Press).

Writing the book required her to visit lots of different forests. She went to New Zealand, Japan, Guatemala, and the Hoh rainforest in the Olympic Peninsula. She was drawn to visit the ancient trees. She spent time in the Hoh with Llyn Roberts (another contributor in this book) and was guided to amazing experiences there.

> I was receiving my own confirmation from Nature. And this magic has continued.

When Julia's book came out, she was doing a lot of book talks. But talking about nature in this magical way was still a bit nerve-wracking for her.

> I thought people would think I was crazy. I felt awkward and vulnerable, talking about this. But, every time, people would come up after my talk to share their own amazing stories about powerful healing experiences.

Recently, while at a friend's house, she noticed some big trees on the property that were marked. Her friend said that they were cutting these down to make room for a greenhouse. Due to her deep connection to trees, she felt their pain over having their lives cut short.

It was then that she suddenly acknowledged a deeper pain within her, resonating with the fate of these trees. At the time she was four months pregnant, and she hadn't realized until that moment that she was afraid of being "cut down," losing herself and her independence, at the prime of her life.

She wondered, *How can I continue to grow into myself and care for another?*

As I have learned from guiding people through nature connection practices, what we notice in nature has some correspondence, or metaphor, within us. It shows us what we might not even be aware that we're feeling. That is where the *aha* moments and deep healing work live.

The fate of the trees thankfully brought to light this unconscious fear she had been holding on to. But now that it was out in the open, she could work with it. And best of all? As soon as she understood this fear, she realized that it's not scary anymore. She can do this. She can be a mother and continue on her spiritual path.

Nature is an amazing mirror into our psyche.

Being connected to the Earth and the land is such a primitive, ancient way of being. Research has discovered the health benefits of gardening, and more importantly, having our bare hands and feet in soil.

Nina seemed to fall into a similar, surprising revelation one afternoon.

> "You are working for me now!"
>
> —Nina Simons

Seeds of Change

Nina Simon's life reached an unexpected fork in the road on a spring afternoon in 1987, while standing in a big open field alongside a garden in southern New Mexico.

She was invited by her filmmaker boyfriend, now husband, Kenny, to visit the master gardener of a farm for his current project. It was a welcome respite from her busy job with the Sante Fe Chamber Music Festival.

> I came along anticipating some time in beautiful nature. Nothing more.

But as they got out of the car, Gabriel Howearth, a cross between a "hippie surfer and biblical prophet," approached them. As they walked through the garden, Gabriel introduced them to the plants, first by their common name and then by their Latin name. And then, he revealed the plant relationships with each member of their plant community. How each member has a supportive and beneficial relationship to each other.

As they walked through this "Garden of Eden," Gabriel invited them to taste the different herbs and fruits, many of which were completely new to Nina. But first, she needed to ask for each plant's permission. It was a garden of relationship, Gabriel explained. Nina saw that he related to these plants as if they were members of his family.

> It was the most magical sensory experience I had ever had. My senses were magnetized, electrified. On a visual level, it was incredibly beautiful. A riot of colors and shapes and forms. An heirloom Elephant Head Amaranth whose scarlet heads, six to seven feet tall, burst into the turquoise sky. Sunflowers, towering overhead with heads over a foot across. I actually felt them watch us as we walked through the garden.
>
> There was a cacophony of pollinators—bees, flies, birds, and butterflies all hovering above rows of plants. There were whole societies of tomatoes—all shapes, sizes, colors, warming in the midday sun. Bursting with the scent of fresh tomatoes.
>
> It was one of the most fertile places I ever experienced in my life. There was more diversity than I had ever seen. It was like they were all dancing together in celebration.

Then Gabriel began to tell them about the impending crisis in the global food supply. How, over the last few decades, many of the small mom and pop seed companies that had been cultivating heirloom and traditional varieties for decades had been bought by big, multinational corporations. And when they did, those corporations stopped cultivating the diversity of seeds, which leads to monocropping.

It came down to one thing for Gabriel—protecting and defending biodiversity, which is nature's failsafe against extinction. Lack of diversity has contributed to so many of the planet's famines, including the Irish Potato Famine in the 1800s.

What evolved was a partnership between Gabriel, Kenny, and a third partner in a seed business, called Seeds of Change. They felt that it was essential for the future of our food supply and life on Earth.

At this point, Nina was struck by this dramatic experience of incredible joy in her body and nervous system. But at the same time, she was horrified by this notion of coming danger.

> Somehow, I knew that he was right. And as we slowly walked back to his house, in sort of a daze, I felt the spirit of the natural world tap me on my shoulder. "You are working for me now!"
>
> I thought, *Oh, no, you've got the wrong girl. I'm a city girl. I don't know anything about farming or business planning.* Up until then, my whole life had been focused on the arts.

But a few days later, Nina realized that this was not a decision for her to make. Her path forward was undeniable. So, she quit her job and became the Director of Marketing for Seeds for Change.

> It was the steepest learning curve of my life, yet one of the most fulfilling. I never felt I had a boss. I was working for nature. It's the closest I've ever felt to direct service to the divine. Nature is sacred.

Nina was raised as an agnostic, assimilating Jew, in New York City. Connection with the Divine, or even talking about it, was not natural for her. But it took that time in the garden to realize that she had always sought nature for solace and guidance.

> I have become more courageous, naming the sacred. The sacred resides in and throughout nature for me.

In the 1980s, organic farms were just beginning, but they had no sources for organic seeds. Nina spent her time negotiating seed contracts, co-creating catalogs, and writing business plans.

> It was a powerful learning time for me. I learned that I could follow my inner guidance instead of heeding self-limiting inner voices. I also found power in admitting what I didn't know and received the support I needed.

Nina sees now that she was being groomed all along. She was no stranger to helping transform people's awareness and consciousness—whether through the arts or environmental and social activism.

Why is it that some vistas capture our attention over others? Perhaps, it's not the vista itself but how open our hearts are when immersed in that landscape. When we stop the mental chatter and allow ourselves to feel the wonder and awe around us, we can hear its messages most clearly. That is what happened to Sylvie on this humble hillside.

> "Yet somehow, it touched me."
>
> —Sylvie Rokab

The Humble Hill

Sylvie Rokab was raised in Rio de Janeiro. Although her family lived in the city, their apartment was on the edge of the mountains. Her parents joyfully nourished her connection to nature from a very early age. Her mother, especially, would sit and watch the clouds as they rolled across the sky, wonder at the tiny world of insects, and participate in the pleasures of the ocean beach.

It was a nearly idyllic, nature-connected childhood.

But when Sylvie was nineteen years old, she had one of her most profound experiences in nature.

During Carnival, a five-day celebration in February, Sylvie and several of her friends decided to escape the madness of the city and retreat to the mountains.

They drove four hours—two of them on rural, nearly empty roads—to reach Mauá, a little village at the heart of the Atlantic Forest of Brazil.

At the time, Sylvie was an undergraduate in economics at a progressive university and was starting to see the reality of a third-world nation. Poverty, corruption, and environmental destruction. Even back in the '80s, Brazil was battling with degradation while ranchers were burning acres of rainforest.

Initially, this trip to Mauá was meant to be all fun. They set up camp in this virgin forest that had no hiking trails. They spent their days hiking and hacking away, creating trails with machetes to discover waterfalls and new vistas. The evenings were filled with campfires, telling stories and singing songs—with some alcohol thrown in, of course.

The forest was filled with incredible, rolling mountains all around, populated by enormous trees and birdsong. Monkeys, macaws, lizards, and insects were around every corner.

The forest was bustling with life.

It was the third day into their trip when, after a bit of lunch, they set out for a new canyon view. It was sunny and warm, with puffy, well-defined clouds passing slowly above.

They got to a vantage point and decided to sit down on the grass to rest and take in the view. While sitting on the hill, Sylvie suddenly noticed that her body had been holding an enormous amount of tension. She hadn't realized how tense she was until it started to melt away on this humble hill.

> This spot wasn't anything more special than any we experienced during the trip. Yet somehow, it touched me. I could hear a waterfall in the distance. There was this rich scent of a forest. Moist soil and mixtures of plants that were warmed by the sun. I can smell it now.

Sylvie hated her economics classes, but she wouldn't let herself quit, and felt she had to finish her degree. She realized all this built-up stress was from her schoolwork, challenges at home, and a developing perspective of the adult world she was now in. Being immersed in the aliveness of the forest, it didn't take long for her to feel peace.

> My senses were awakened. It really felt like magic!
> I realized that, if I can feel my pain disappear into nothingness, I knew nature could be healing for everyone. It was medicine for me. And it could be medicine for anyone. It felt so powerful and wonderous. I knew then that someday, I would help awaken people to this same realization. But I was an undergrad in economics! I had no idea what that would look like.

She realized that most people are so incredibly disconnected from nature. They often don't realize that their separation causes personal suffering. But on a larger scale, too. We are often disconnected from everything that nourishes us in body, mind, and spirit.

> Everyone needs to have that connection to their source, the source of everything. Civilization itself is causing catastrophes. Entire communities are unable to drink their water, are breathing polluted air, and are ingesting foods filled with pesticides from depleted soils.
> The whole ecology of human society is breaking down from climate change, threatening to completely unravel civilization. I had a sense that this was a significant moment in my life. My adult life was just starting. I understood that each of us make ripples. It was an experience that powerfully moved me in a direction that I wasn't aware of previously.

When they finally left the forest, the ride home started out on the empty rural roads and then, increasingly, paved roads crowded with vehicles and people. Sylvie shared that she felt overwhelmed by the sounds and the incredibly violent, aggressive energy of the city.

> We went from a harmonious symphony of life to these rivers of metal, glass, and machinery. One quote that I love that has helped me come back into harmony is by Alan Watts, "You didn't come into this world, you came out of it like a wave from the ocean."

Sylvie's mother is a mystical soul. She gifted her such a beautiful worldview. They were driving together a few months ago in Miami and were both commenting on a cloud ahead that was morphing shapes and shades of color, from white to dark gray.

> It was so delightful and joyful! And we laughed!

Sylvie returned to the small village of Mauá when she was filming her award-winning documentary, *Love Thy Nature*. She was grateful to see that the village was still sleepy and sweet.

> It was odd, because, although I loved it being quiet and slow, the filmmaker/producer part of me was impatient.

They had a limited window to film: the magical time just after dawn and right before sunset. But the villagers slept late. Breakfast wasn't ready until eight thirty! It required her to go inward and come back into balance.

> I recognized the foundation of the truth that we have forgotten. By being in nature, we come back to our true selves.

It's interesting that one of the last stories that I recorded was with someone that I'm very close with. And to hear her story was one of the most unexpected and personally more profound for me. I smile, because I realize that magic is just around the corner at any time in our lives, even when we least expect it.

"This is who you are. This is what you need to do in your life."

—Janine Bendickson

A Second Chance

Janine Bendickson was that kid that thought her life's mission was to save the wildlife in her neighborhood. She was closer to her calling at eight years old than she was at thirty.

"I would stand in my yard and sing to the birds. I remember singing 'Somewhere Over the Rainbow,' and they would sing with me!" At least that's what she imagined.

She would find small animals and build them a home in her yard. And because some of her charges died under care, Janine took on the responsibility of giving these animals a proper burial. In fact, she would search her neighborhood for dead birds and small mammals and bury them in her yard.

During one of these funerals, Janine recalls something magical that happened.

> After I placed the bird in the hole and covered it with dirt, I tapped my foot on top of the dirt, and I heard the bird sing! I thought I had buried it alive! I quickly dug it up and it was still dead, no life at all. So I placed it back in the ground, tapped my foot on the dirt, and again, I heard the bird sing!

She believed that she was communicating with an enchanted world, where you could speak with animals. This was a sign that nature was thanking her for her care and effort. Even then, she felt a strong sense of spiritual connection with these animals.

As she grew older and retold this story to others, she realized the science behind this experience. When she tapped her foot above the bird, oxygen was released that was trapped in the birds' lungs, sounding like birdsong. But even now, she smiles, with curiosity and an open mind.

Later, Janine went to college and got her BA. She got married, had two children, and started her own business creating art pieces that she would sell at craft shows.

But then she got sick. While going through treatments for Stage III cancer, she decided to take a job as curator for Sweetbriar Nature Center, which offered local nature education to schools, scouts, and the public.

> At that time, my life turned upside down. I was trying to find myself again. Even now, my ex-husband (since divorced) says that Sweetbriar saved me.

She loved reestablishing her connection with nature and animals, and teaching children about the environment. Then, one day, she realized that there was more to Sweetbriar. She saw that they had a wildlife rehabilitation area.

She suddenly felt her childhood flood back in. It was magnetic. She knew that she had to be there, in the rehabilitation work.

> A voice inside me urged, *This is who you are. This is what you need to do in your life.*
>
> I knew I had to learn how to care for these animals. To learn the correct housing and food. What they needed to not only survive, but to thrive. Inside, I knew that I was going to make this happen.

Despite never being much of a test taker in school, Janine got 100 percent on her wildlife rehab test.

> I never felt so good before about taking a test. This test, man, was so simple, I knew all the answers! For so many years, I had no idea that a job like this existed. And somehow, I was brought right to it when I needed it most.

I asked Janine the moment she knew her calling when she was working at Sweetbriar.

I was sitting around my kitchen with Marie, the director, and Nancy, one of my colleagues. We were feeding baby rabbits. We had the right food, syringes, and the proper technique.

I remember having this moment like, *Oh my gosh, is this real? A bunch of women, baby rabbits...* I knew this is what I had to do with my life. Something in my heart, my soul, telling me that these animals needed me.

I realize now that any animal that comes into our rehab center would be dead in the wild without our help. Whatever we do for them—so that they can hopefully be released back into the wild—is a second chance.

For me, it's all about second chances. I was saved by my work at Sweetbriar. Before that, running my business was so stressful. I made good money, but it was evidently killing me.

Helping these animals has given me a second chance in my life. And if I can do that for them, that fills my heart. I do the best I can for them. I'm always learning about new techniques and resources to improve their chances for survival and release.

But there is a limit to what rehabilitation can do. Is it better to keep an animal alive and live in captivity if it cannot be released to the wild? What is best for this animal if they cannot experience the wild and what it's like to be free?

But when they come into our care and we interact with them every day, we see that they have unique personalities. They are individuals, just like you and I.

Janine told me about a blue jay named Marguerite. She came into Sweetbriar as a baby and was raised by humans. She had become imprinted—meaning that she saw no difference between herself and humans. She chose Janine to be her "partner."

I experienced firsthand what it's like to be a bird in love. She kept me safe from other predators—safe from other humans! She would

> attack people that came too close to me! Choosing a partner is a big decision for an animal. They won't pick just anybody.
>
> She would find the best food around and feed my hand, as if it were the mouth of another bird. She would sleep on my shoulder and just wanted to be with me.

Marguerite was at Sweetbriar for roughly ten years, which is a long life for a blue jay.

When she died, it was very difficult for Janine. Her death was unexpected. Marguerite loved bathing all day long. And that's where Janine found her. In the turtle bath.

> When any animal passes, especially one that's been an ambassador, I'm always sad. But that connection with her was so strong. It was one of the hardest passings of any animal I've worked with there.
>
> I still see her there in rehab. I'll be opening the water tray and imagine her scooping down to get drinks of water. It happens all the time. Being so close with her was a wonderful experience.

Marguerite is buried at Sweetbriar with a little tombstone.

> These animals have so many of the same emotions we have. I always thought that was true. That they had consciousness, but I didn't know for sure. Now I can attest to it.

So many people ask Janine if she believes that these animals know that they are helping them.

> Mostly, no. We are predators to them. They are frightened of us. But I will say that when we released this bald eagle, that was here for a few days recently, back to the wild, there was a moment when he turned around and looked at us for a split second, as if he was acknowledging our help. He knew.
>
> Even a wild coyote that was brought in for a few weeks ran about twenty feet away when he was released, stopped and

looked back at us, and then went off into the woods. There is consciousness and connection there.

Janine ended our conversation with this revelation:

> It wasn't until I was reviewing your questions that I realized all of this. I love telling stories, but I never saw or felt the thread through it all. That what I was doing as a child was a call to my purpose in this life.
>
> But now it's all come together. It's pretty astonishing how I never saw it before!

Invitation: Aimless Wandering

As Llyn Roberts did in her story, go aimlessly wandering in a natural place. Let yourself "wander with wonderment, with heart and senses open, and with no destination or purpose other than to appreciate and be open to nature."

Feel the gentle movements of your body as you walk, relaxed and open. Let yourself be spontaneously guided. No agenda or destination. Have a question in mind regarding your purpose or calling. Perhaps you are asking for messages on what it is, or to confirm that you're on the right path, or what your next step should be. Invite whatever wants to communicate with you, be it the breeze, a bird, or a rock. As always, after your experience, journal about your experience.

CHAPTER 8

Rites of Passage

～

*"Remind me that the most fertile lands
were built by the fires of volcanoes."*

—Andrea Gibson

～

In this modern world, we've lost the richness of the sacred ritual of initiation. In my experience, many religious rituals today lack the deep spiritual connection with the divine that was once central to the human transformative experience. If we are to become spiritually awakened, we must create new initiation processes, finding alternative ways to foster that connection.

These rites of passage are most-often experienced when we go through great challenges, or even traumatic events, in our lives. Near-fatal illness and near-death experiences are two ways that can stir these awakening experiences. But that doesn't necessarily mean we will emerge from the ordeal with greater wisdom and enlightenment. We must do the work.

These experiences are typified in three phases: severance, threshold, and integration. We sever from our ordinary life, and often from our loved ones. We step through a doorway to an experience, with trials and challenges, and then we emerge and are tasked to integrate our learnings to form a new perspective, worldview, and perhaps recognize a new personal mythology.

This chapter contains stories of spiritual initiations, which we may experience more than once in our lifetimes.

> "As I got older, I couldn't hear them sing anymore.
> But I never forgot that I could."
>
> —Amos Clifford

The Medicine of Poison Oak

Amos Clifford's first memory is of lying in his crib in Santa Barbara. The morning sun would light up the landscape. He remembers hearing the trees sing. "Oranges! Oranges! Lemons!" they seemed to say in his small ear. Other trees would also be singing, but he couldn't understand what they said, as if it was a different language.

> We get trained out of this ability early in life. As I got older, I couldn't hear them sing anymore. But I never forgot that I could.

However, Amos discovered other ways to communicate with trees as he got older.

As a child, he roamed free in the hills and valleys of the Santa Barbara area. He would often sneak into the botanical garden and explore. Possessing a terrible allergy to poison oak since childhood, when he was sixteen, he encountered a large stand of poison oak in those hills, probably forty feet deep. He spontaneously decided to make peace with it.

> I talked to the poison oak and told it that I was so tired of the rashes. And it talked back to me. I heard the poison oak respond, but not with my physical ears—with my inner ears.

What he heard it say was, "if you're really serious about this, show how trusting you are by walking through us." Amos walked through the patch and didn't get the rash. That immunity lasted for forty years. "And when my immunity stopped, it was very harsh medicine."

Amos participated in a yearlong soul initiation process for men, where they spent time at a ranch in a steep mountainous area in California.

There was a lot of poison oak in the area, and although Amos took precautions while working on the land in the summer heat, it eventually caught up with him.

> I got poison oak on my laces and then my hands. Without realizing this, of course, I ate with my hands, and that was a nightmare.

The poison oak got inside his body. For the next three weeks, his entire body was covered in blisters and shedding his skin. He was in incredible pain.

He wondered why he had a reaction to the poison again after all these years—and such a bad case. He knew there had to be a lesson. He sat and meditated on this for a while.

> It didn't take long for me to realize that poison oak was supporting my initiation process. It was helping me transform from the outside in. Shedding my skin so that a new man could emerge.

His story serves as a powerful but painful metaphor for transformation and the extinction of our old ways, beliefs, and perspectives on ourselves and the world.

During the challenge, or ordeal, required for spiritual transformation, our senses are heightened. We are more fully in our bodies. One colleague called it becoming a "full spectrum" human. Gordon, although acutely aware and focused on hearing, found that being in the wild, alone and vulnerable, opened his senses like never before.

"Here is the silence that is beneath everything."

—Gordon Hempton

Ccaen'tsu Daja—Let It Happen

The "soundtracker" Gordon Hempton has a "quiver of so many transformative places" in his life. Which one does he choose to share? I prefer my interviewees just go with their gut, knowing that whatever story arises wants to be heard.

> I am a listener of vanishing natural soundscapes on a planet with eight billion people. When I get to a place with quiet, natural environments, I usually find out why people aren't there! There's lots of pain and suffering and endangerment in those places. Sometimes also disappointment. All are ingredients for wonderful epiphanies.

Gordon asserts that sight is not the most important sense. He asks, "If sight is so important for survival, how come we only have eyes at the front of our head? We can close our eyes, but our ears never sleep. They are essential for survival."

> As so many audiologists believe, our ears are not tuned to human voices. They are tuned to birdsong because that is the number one indicator of a prosperous land. Places with flowing water, edible plants, and insects are places that we can survive as well. To fall in love with place, we have to listen.

For the last four decades, Gordon's goal has remained to be a better listener. He has hearing aids today and that has led him to the revelation that even a deaf person can listen. They can listen to how they feel, letting the world in through all their senses. By listening with thought, without words, we can notice how we feel.

He shares that Americans are a homeless culture. We are cut off from our land, our place. There is so much noise pollution in our towns and cities. We isolate indoors, away from the world in an attempt to control our environment.

> But controlling our environment is not going to challenge and inform us. Let's stop and listen to our quiet space for a moment. You can feel peaceful and safe. It's certainly much better than noise pollution. We cannot hear indicators of prosperity that we evolved to detect. We cannot hear the natural soundscape.
>
> So here is my story. I didn't expect it to be my story today. But this conversation has led me to choose this one.

In 2010, Gordon was speaking at a Ted X event, where he met Randy Boorman, chief of the Cofan Tribe in Ecuador.

> He was a modern-day Tarzan. He was born and raised in the tribe. He eventually became a shaman and chief and married the most knowledgeable person on the healing properties of Amazon plants.

According to Randy, indigenous people listen in the jungle to find food and hear warnings of danger. Gordon found that the tribe has no words for love or sacred in their language. "Why divide what is loved and not loved, or sacred and not? They also didn't have a word for adventure because they believe that all of life is an adventure. Especially if you live in the Amazon."

Randy offered to have Gordon return with him to spend time with the Cofan. So, two years later, Gordon arrived with his son and daughter to experience the Cofan's homeland.

While there, the Cofan offered the opportunity to do a solo journey in the Amazon.

As we were preparing to go, I leaned over to one of my companions, who leads a transformational travel council. I said something like, "This may be our last conversation perhaps ever! I feel like they are leading an innocent baby into the jungle and abandoning them. Anything can happen." I remember he laughed back at me and said "yay, I know!"

Gordon was then led by an elder on foot, "on a path that I could not see, but they could."

While I was with my guide, I was instructed to do exactly as he did. You step where they step. When you see them step aside to avoid a branch, you will do that. It is sustained present moment awareness. There is no time or temptation to be distracted by even a thought of the modern world. The center of biodiversity is where you learn your place in life. We are not on top of the food chain, we are merely on it.

We constructed a shelter from jungle resources. We built a fire, started by resinous debris left by a beetle. He added a tropical log so the fire would burn all night.

Then, he left me. He walked away.

My ears became fully alive. I heard layers of insects, the last calls of the birds, the low sound of the Caymans, a crocodile-like animal who snaps their jaws shut to communicate to each other across the river.

Being alone in this place changed my view of the world. I was just there, being in my being. Listening for the first time, all alone, two hours from the closest human being. I was listening to what may literally be the last place on Earth that we might describe as Eden. No chainsaw marks, no roads, not even a human footprint. Just listening.

At first, admittedly, he realized that he was afraid. He felt fear. But he listened. Kept listening. And he noticed the countless insects, frogs, the forest wildlife that have no names—some of which have not even been identified by science. He was listening to something that can best be described as the inner workings of God's clock.

> Everything was so precise and interwoven. And I felt like I was inside of that super being. My soul dissolved and disappeared, and with that, so did fear. It was the moment that I finally arrived on planet Earth.
>
> And with that, I laid down in my shelter and went to sleep. I listened all night long to the beautiful deep music that we cannot create. I can document the concert with my recording devices, but I cannot create this living miracle. This live concert was irreplaceable, even by a recording.

When he awoke in the morning, he was surprised!

> I woke up and thought about how the night before, I was ready to die. Ready to die in this perfect place. I submitted myself and found my place. And at this moment, I thought, *I'm still alive! Isn't that wonderful?*
>
> My spirituality was truly born that morning.

He did have a cell phone. Not that it would help communicate with anyone in the rainforest, but he took a picture of himself that morning before his Cofan guide arrived. He stood in front of the shelter. There was no need to smile or have any emotion except for deep reverence.

The guide came back around midday, and they nodded hello.

On the way back, Gordon had a profound realization that he was living life incredibly wrong. He realized that he had thought the only way to have something happen was to make it happen. So upon returning to camp, he asked Randy, "Is there a Cofan expression for 'to let it happen'?"

> The Amazon taught me that when we are grounded in the universe, you never make anything happen. You let it happen.

I realized that my Western viewpoint was such an arrogant view of our relationship to the world. I realized that I need to be more mindful, less hurried, to take a half step back, to observe with all of my senses. Observe what is already happening. That we are always within a super being. Then, you move forward with your awareness with it.

Randy's reply was, "Oh yes! It's *Ccaen'tsu Daja* [pronounced kaa-en-stew-daha]. It's the indigenous way of life. Why would you live any other way?"

Before boarding his plan to go home, Gordon had that phrase tattooed on his right forearm, "so that, when I find myself trying to make things happen, I recall that the flow of what is already is."

When I reach to make something happen, I see those words, then relax my grip. I take a step back and observe. I've applied this to both my personal and professional life. I have achieved so much more than I ever thought I would. It's a way of life that is easily forgotten in the rush of modern life.

In living this way of life, I found the most important thing to pay attention to is how you feel. You don't need to describe it, give it words, or even think about it. Just acknowledge you feel this way. My mother told me there are three points to remember for success in life: be yourself, do your best—always do your best—and accept whatever happens from that because this is the life God intended you to live.

We are still our ancestors. We do our best thinking and make the best use of our senses in places that our senses can apprehend information and make sense of life. My definition of noise pollution is very simple: relatively loud, simple sound that denies us access to subtle, meaningful sounds.

The vibration of noise pollution is destroying our very ability to make sense of the world and find meaning. It is shaking our thoughts apart.

> We need to be in nature, to have it all come together. To understand why we are here, how each person is so unique and needed to be here on the planet.

The land in the Amazon where the Cofan live is now called the Zabalo River Wilderness Quiet Park, the first of its kind, designated by Quiet Parks International, which Gordon helped found.

> I return to the Amazon two or three times a year. It's my church. I go there and come back feeling refreshed, invigorated, and back in the world.
>
> Here is the silence that is beneath everything.

The silence beneath everything. How profoundly Gordon pulled me into the experience of his story of the Amazon rainforest. I found myself yearning to be there to witness that vast oneness of sound. But this next story brought me back to childhood.

How many of us experienced a sense of oneness as a child? It's unlikely that it happens much these days, but a few decades ago, this contributor shared her shift of consciousness at a sleepaway camp.

> "This was the initiation of my soul."
>
> —Jean Shinoda Bolen

Initiation of My Soul

Every summer, Jungian analyst and prolific author Jean Shinoda Bolen, MD, would attend Girl Scout Camp at Camp Osito at Big Bear Lake. She grew up in Los Angeles and was never able to see the stars at night. There was always smog and city lights.

It was a rough-it-type of camp. Each unit had a big tent and they slept outdoors every night, under the Jeffersonian pines. They smelled of sweet vanilla. Tucked into a sleeping bag on a cot, Jean was lulled to sleep by the night sounds.

> I would shift around in my sleeping bag until I finally landed on my back and looked up. I recall the majesty of the Milky Way right above me. There's something about being up in the mountains, going to sleep under the Milky Way every single night, looking up at the sky. I'd never seen that before, growing up in LA. I would just lie there and appreciate the gorgeousness.

Perhaps it was the second or third time that she went, she recalls feeling something different. This one night, there was a slight shift of consciousness.

> I looked up, and wow. At once, there was a feeling, a sense, that I was part of the Milky Way. It was as if my spirit rose to join it. I wasn't separate from it. It was deep within me.

Born to Japanese-American parents, Jean attended Presbyterian Sunday school every week. Her parents were both college-educated and, in fact, her mother was a physician. But despite her parents' scientific views, this form of religion was still based in a literal translation of the Bible and patriarchy.

With this experience, Jean realized that connection with the universe was real.

But her learned beliefs did not prepare her for this experience, a sense of participating as a part of this amazing universe. It was awe-inspiring.

Psychologist C.G. Jung wrote about the idea of the larger Self. Jean shared this concept with me.

> When younger, our ego connects and is influenced by life happenings. But as you grow older and wiser on the spiritual path, you realize that the ego is not in charge. That was parallel

to what I experienced at the age of nine. Being connected to the universe, and no longer just my little self. The universe is beautiful and amazing, and I was a part of it.

Jean shares her decades-long interest in subjects related to psychology, parapsychology, and reincarnation. They are related. All just different ways of looking at where we are, a sense of being young and old souls, and connected to our purpose.

"As an old soul, we have a purpose here and now... I believe this was the initiation of my soul, becoming one with the universe. It left a deep impression on me still to this day." This experience was part of her purpose in life.

We are raised developing our left brain only. Our right brain—our intuitive, spiritual nature—is so often dismissed.

In recent times, with the melting of glaciers, temperatures over 110 degrees, wildfires, and drought, there is great potential for us.

Women, and those closer to nature, realize that we are part of this divinity. We have been gifted this planet. As we speak, we are about to launch another space mission to the moon. It's named Artemis, which is the name of my last book! The goddess, Artemis, is showing us that men and women need to come together. We have to work together and be part of this beautiful world we've been given.

There is a focal point right now. Everything seems to be coming to a head. The combination of extreme planetary weather, and now Artemis, with the ability to, yet again, see the earth from outer space. For the first time in history, the Artemis mission plans for a woman to walk on the moon. Artemis is the twin sister of Apollo (the mission that landed on the moon fifty years ago) and is the mythological goddess of the moon. She is curious and confident with a sense of adventure, and is connected with wildlife, trees, childbirth, and all of nature.

Artemis has the potential for awakening the goddess within all of us.

Like Jean Shinoda Bolen, one of my first awakening experiences was while camping as a child. But this one took years to integrate. In fact, writing this book inspired me to penetrate a story that I've recounted a few times to close friends over the years. And yes, much greater meaning was uncovered.

> "...have I no experience from childhood to share?"
>
> —Maureen Calamia

A Lightning Initiation

The rain started softly at first. Then it fell as if it had some vengeance to mete out on the soil.

Anyone who has gone tent camping knows the deafening sound of rain on canvas, which I have come to love. But this night was my first experience. In fact, it was my first of many experiences.

It was dark and I was unable to stop my mind from racing. I felt strange and alone in my new denim sleeping bag. It was decidedly mature—unlike the Holly Hobby ones some of my friends had at sleepovers—and cool—but not like "temperature" cool. In fact, it was a rather hot material for an August night on the beach!

I would have flung the bag open to get some air if it weren't for my fear.

Never mind that my best friend was just inches from me. She could have been a mile away.

Then, with a sudden jolt, thunder and lightning crashed, and I realized there was only a thin piece of fabric separating me from the terrifying forces of nature.

The thunder seemed to echo my alarm.

I felt exposed and vulnerable, but my eleven-year-old self could not put it into those exact words.

Lightning struck the earth, just like it had struck my life just six weeks prior.

My father died suddenly on June 23, 1974. At least his death was sudden for me. Seems that everyone else knew it was coming, including my older siblings. I was still in shock. My school year had just ended, and I was excited for the summer. He died a few days later.

That summer was surreal, turned upside down. During the course of everyday life, and everyday situations, I would temporarily forget. Only to suddenly recall my recent fate.

My father is dead.

My friend's mother, obviously looking to help ease my pain with a new experience, invited me to join them on their annual camping vacation on the beach in Montauk, NY.

A beach on the ocean was one of my favorite places in the whole wide world. The beach for a whole week was a dream come true! My mom approved.

And this night was the very first night I was ever away from my family. The first night I slept in a tent. And the first night I felt helpless amongst the fury of the natural world.

And then *it* happened.

At first, I thought that I had peed in my pants. There was a warm gush in my sleeping bag. *What was going on?* I managed to get my friend to accompany me to the camp restroom. We pulled on our sweatshirts and grabbed something to cover our heads and ran.

In the complete darkness of the beach, interrupted by occasional illumination from lightning, we ran toward the light.

And then I saw, and recognized, my very first experience as a woman, according to traditional cultures. My first menstruation.

Shock again.

And then humiliation. My friend, two years older than me, had not gotten hers yet. I was so ashamed and embarrassed!

Indigenous cultures have rites of passage to formally initiate a child to adulthood. The first menses biologically represents this transition. But in our modern world, there isn't any ritual or ceremony, nor any process that helps in this shift.

I was at the most vulnerable point in my life. I see now that my carefree youth was gone.

Over the years, I have not shared this memory often, as you can imagine. I've told it only a few times in my life. So, having seen little "daylight," the significance of my story had not been given much thought.

The deeper symbolism of this experience only became apparent when I was preparing for this book. As I probed my life for awe-inspiring experiences to recount, I kept being guided to my adulthood. I thought, *Have I no experience from childhood to share?*

As this memory rose to the surface of my consciousness, I started writing it down. It wasn't coming together, so I left it for a month or so. As I sit here now, I see so much more than what initially was there.

It was as though the lightning was within my body. The lightning struck deep inside and forever changed me. I felt more alone, separate. But more importantly, I feel that I was marked—or rather, "illuminated."

Indeed, the symbolism of lightning has visited me throughout my life.

In my late thirties, I was going through what some would call a "midlife crisis." Each area of my life—career, marriage, home life—was being turned upside down. I was being called to do something more meaningful in my life.

Around this time, I started paying more attention to my dreams. They seemed to guide me in my everyday life.

One night, lightning made an appearance in a profound way. I had a dream, an Epic Dream, in which I was struck by a lightning bolt. And my body was suspended two feet in the air. As I floated there, unable to move, I wondered if I was dead. But then I woke up.

A few years later, when sharing this dream with a shaman, he gave me deep wisdom into my past and my calling. It was then that I realized that a lightning strike was not only to initiate a shaman but to deepen their skills and their divine connections. It was meant to be a grand light switch either in waking or dreaming life. And since then, I've had several dreams of being struck.

With all my connections to lightning, I believe that contemplation of the symbolism and metaphors of life provides a richer, deeper experience of life that can help us understand who we are. Awesome childhood experiences of nature are just the beginning. We are open to the wonder and curiosity of the natural world and our place within it.

So many of us did not awaken to the sacredness of nature until later in life. Despite spending her entire childhood on a farm, this story is how Sonja was awakened by another experience which has forever changed her perspective on life.

> "I felt so many layers of the experience at once."
>
> —Sonja Bochart

Cultivating Nature Experience

Although Sonja Bochart grew up on a farm, among cows, horses, goats, and expansive views, it wasn't until she was in her thirties that she can recall a profound experience in nature.

But first, earlier that year, she was finishing her five-hundred-hour yoga teacher training and was auditing classes to observe and take notes. At the end of one of these classes, the students went into the final pose called savasana, or corpse pose, to integrate energy and movement during the class. The teacher moved around the room, gently placing his hands on each student, in quiet presence.

As Sonja sat at the back of the room observing, she was suddenly aware of an interchange of energy between teacher and student. That he was "holding space" for each of them.

> I had awareness that he opened his heart—energetically. I was unexpectedly moved to tears.

She watched as the teacher cradled the weight of their heads in his hands, as if he was in communion with the weight of their beings. Just witnessing without judgement or criticism. With immense presence and compassion.

The energy was palpable. It resonated deeply within her, in her heart. She felt a greater knowing about our interconnectedness with all. There was amazing care that this gesture communicated.

> I took yoga training to learn yoga, its theories, and the correctness of asana [poses] and pranayama [breath], to help us create greater health in body, mind, and spirit. But that day, I learned the true sacredness of the practice.

Later that year, she traveled to Hawaii with her partner. He suggested scuba diving lessons.

Sonja was terrified at first, but she decided to rise to the challenge.

After a couple of days of lessons, she found herself in the ocean, about forty feet deep.

> I was on my back and looked up. I could see the intense current of the ocean crash into the rocks above. I could feel the impact and power of the waves. Yet, at the same moment, I felt an immense calm, softness, peace, and sense of oneness.

It was a completely new visual perspective for Sonja, and it, again, shifted her worldview.

> Suddenly, I felt so many layers of the experience at once; the strength and power of the ocean, the sunlight rippling through the blue water above. Such beauty, peacefulness.
>
> And in addition to all the visual sights was the quality of sound. We experience sounds so differently when submerged.
>
> It was quiet and soft, almost like hushed voices in a cathedral. It was reverent.
>
> I felt that same moment as I did in yoga class—so deeply connected. I felt that I was waking up to the truth of interconnectedness.

While interviewing others for this book, I have found that most of my participants lived in the countryside or spent their summers in nature as children. And so did Sonja. She was always outdoors as a child.

So, I wondered, *why did it take a yoga class to awaken her to this deep connection to the natural world?*

> I don't think I could experience a deep connection to nature until I could truly experience it in my own body. I don't believe that I was fully "here" until that moment in yoga.

As a child she took the farm for granted. She was in such a hurry to grow up and go to the big city that she didn't appreciate nature all around her, every day.

> I believe that I was guided on this path so I could get this perspective. So, I could see the extremes of rural and urban living. I love cities, and community, but after living there for a few decades, I could see that the lack of nature contributed to many urban problems.

Sonja pursued her growing passion for nature and design. She became one of the first consultants on biophilic design (a.k.a. bringing nature indoors) and finds that weaving natural patterns through our buildings can help people foster greater connection, not only with nature, but with each other.

> At its best, biophilic design can provide a fuller expression of our lives. It adds layers to our experience. It can get us out of our heads, into our hearts. And by doing this, we will hopefully be kinder to ourselves and others; more generous and loving. Life is hard right now. I really think we need those connections with nature in our lives.
>
> People can talk about connection, but you just have to experience it in your own way. No one can tell you how to feel it. That personal connection encouraged me to be more open and receptive in the natural world.

Sonja shared a recent study on biophilic design's ability to enhance empathy and compassion. The results found that people who experienced nature in groups and shared their stories had more impactful experiences in nature.

Perhaps, when sharing our stories with others, we give ourselves permission to experience more deeply. And this may be a result of more open hearts and a feeling of community.

In my personal experience, forest bathing therapy does just this. We go out as a group, participate in a few open invitations to connect with nature, and then have the opportunity to share with others. It's not unlike what indigenous people have done for thousands of years, while sitting in a circle around a campfire.

When we start to heal ourselves, we heal our relationships and heal the Earth.

While we were doing the interview, Sonja smiled as she noticed a small lizard on the fence in her garden.

> We don't necessarily need that experience in Hawaii, like I had. Even the smallest ones are important. We have to be intentional and present. We are usually in a state of fight or flight. Striving

to do better, go faster, spend less, and be more innovative. What we need is more mindfulness, connection, meditative practices like yoga, and nature connection.

I strongly believe in what Kellert said [Stephen Kellert, author and former professor of social ecology at Yale University]. Being in union with nature is inherent biologically within us. But it needs to be fostered and cultivated, just like yoga practice. Now, I can come outside for a short while and reconnect. I can have moments of awe watching that lizard. It just takes the simplest things to shift us. But, for some, it takes some time to open up to that.

Invitation: Turning Points

Reflect on the turning points in your life. Not the traditional ones, such as graduation, getting married, or moving into your first home—although these can accompany metaphysical turning points, as well.

Consider a time when something occurred that was shocking or surprising, but curious as well.

I am hoping that a story shared in this chapter brought up a memory for you to explore in greater detail.

Consider if there was anything that preceded this shift, such as time in nature, or a specific experience or encounter of a natural kind.

Were you somehow separated from your everyday routines and acquaintances? Did you "step" through the threshold willingly or unwillingly? Were you able to integrate that experience into your life, resulting in a shift in your worldview or perspective?

Recall as much detail as possible about this experience. What occurred before and after. Recall any dreams associated with this experience. Try to recall as much as you can about how you felt in your physical body and senses.

Journal about this experience.

CHAPTER 9

The "Super" Natural in Waking Life

"We could not live our lives on the ecstatic level of the sacred...the daily business of living would never get done. There does, however, come a time when one must learn to move between the two ways of 'seeing' reality in order to become a whole person."

—**Malidoma Patrice Somé,** *Of Water and the Spirit*

Malidoma speaks of two ways of "seeing" reality. Many of us are experiencing these openings to the sacred, yet we still need to stay firmly grounded. Like a tree, we must remain rooted while reaching for the stars.

In conversations with the contributors to this book, I discovered that some of their stories may seem, to some, like mere tales—too fantastical to be real. But let us not forget one crucial message from nature: consciousness saturates everything we see and all that remains unseen.

Some people spoke about keeping these stories to themselves, all these years. Some even doubted their sanity. And this makes me wonder how many people have had "wild" experiences but were afraid to voice them?

To speak our deep truths requires a fair amount of courage. My guess is that there are many more stories than we will ever hear.

Following are a series of experiences shared by a few brave souls. I felt that it was fitting to call them "super" natural. Perhaps you have a story of your own.

> "But for me, well, it helped me to experience the parting of the veils, that is connecting to the spiritual realm."
>
> —Les Stroud

Hearing the Mountains

Although Les Stroud is known worldwide as the "Survivorman," the essence of his life's work is not just about surviving in nature but reminding people about the importance of connecting to the natural world for greater well-being in body, mind, and spirit.

> Spending time in nature through activities—like cross-country skiing, kayaking, even running in the hills—is not "it."
> Using nature for an activity, or to get in shape, that's not connecting to nature.

Les is a big proponent of forest bathing and other earth-based practices.

"To me, this is what it's all about," he told me. "Even the love songs that I write *are* about the love and longing for nature."

He said that, like many of us, he grew up in a dysfunctional family with issues of mental illness among family members. "I learned as a teenager that nature was always there for me, when others were not."

I asked Les to share a story of revelation or epiphany. He shared that he doesn't believe in sudden revelations.

> I have always seen it as a process. Maybe more like Malcom Gladwell's "tipping point." There could be years of slow growth, a flattish curve upward. Then an event where everything comes to light that's true—however, it is the long flattish curve that is where the real change happens.

That is what he has experienced. A slow build-up of knowing and then, *seemingly* all of a sudden, an awakening to something new. It's more about looking back at all that has happened and finally making sense of it in that one "epiphany" moment.

Between 2009 and 2010, Les produced his own series, *Beyond Survival* and spent a year traveling the world, living with remote indigenous cultures who live close to the earth. He slept where they slept, ate what they ate, engaged in their activities, including deeply held ceremonies that keep them close to the earth. "I call it my yearlong vision quest."

While filming these ten separate documentaries, Les found that some tribes were more heart-based and authentic than others. And it was with those people where the ceremonies were most profound.

> I tend to be a stubborn person, more skeptical and cynical than others might think. I approach these cultures and practices with a bit of that cynicism. And some of these people were filled with what I would call loving, feminine energy.

One tribe in Indonesia were pure animists, Les recalls. They believe that everything is sentient: the tree, the salamander, the rock on the path. They lived in accordance with their beliefs.

With a tribe in Peru, Les participated in a plant medicine ceremony with San Pedro, a cactus.

> Unlike ayahuasca, which takes you on a journey down into yourself, this experience with San Pedro was about profoundly connecting to nature.

> Don't misunderstand me about hallucinogens. These ceremonies are not to be entered into lightly, or uninformed. There is a process of fasting and purifying the body for weeks beforehand. I was guided by a mentor. Believe me, you are not getting high! However, I believe these plant experiences (I have done ayahuasca as well) really helped me break through my obstinacy and let it all flow. I'm not the type to meditate. And I do realize that not everyone needs plant medicines to have these experiences. But for me, well, it helped me to experience the parting of the veils that *is* connecting to the spiritual realm.

He continued to discuss what he learned from his time with plant medicine.

> When I drank San Pedro with that Peruvian shaman, it was really powerful. I remember lying there and suddenly hearing a female voice from behind my head. I realized that this was the voice of Panchama, the voice of Mother Earth. We proceeded to have a profound conversation. She said, "A long time ago, we were lovers. We were in love. You've been away, but you've finally come back to me. So, pull up a chair and let's talk."
>
> I immediately knew what she meant.
>
> When I was around twenty years old, I was an outdoor guide. I was always outside and very connected to the land. Everything I did was about nature. I would fall asleep on a rock by river, I would kiss the ground when I awoke and say, "Thank you!" But strangely, at that time, I wasn't clued into the metaphysical part of connection. So, when she said that—I knew what she meant. I was out in nature a lot (hey, I was Survivorman!) but I wasn't engaging in dialogues with her. I wasn't listening.

Les explained that this experience was so stunning and real. It was as if he were talking to an old, wise friend.

During that trip, while traversing the mountains, there were members of the tribe that were out ahead of the group. Their role was, in essence, to clear the way for their passage. But not in a physical sense. As they walked, they asked the mountains ahead for their permission to proceed, for their support. And only when they received that would they move onward.

Although Les understood this practice on a superficial level, he did not comprehend how they received "permission" from the land.

A year later, Les found himself back filming *Survivorman* and was on Tiburon Island, the largest island in Mexico, in the Gulf of California. As usual, he was camping out on his own, with a backpack filled with camera equipment and a few items, but no food or water.

"I was in the middle of this ten-day shoot, moving from the coast to go inland," he said. "Of course, I was alone. The safety crew is always a few miles away. That night I camped out in the best place I could find. It was a wide, flat space with rocks and scrub desert brush. That morning when I awoke, I noticed lots of broken shards of pottery. I found out later that this spot was considered sacred to the local people."

By midday, he was walking toward these small mountains, more like foothills, across this flat expanse.

> I remember the weather was idyllic. Blue sky, sunny, and the air was calm. Going forward on all of my treks ever since I met the Peruvian tribe, I made it a custom to ask for permission as I walked through the land. I was showing my respect, but never got a response. Because of the great risks I took filming each episode, it made sense for me to get all the help I could!

But this time was different.

> When I asked permission, a cacophony of sound washed over me. I heard a chorale of voices answer back! Not only a group, but I could actually hear individual voices. They were young, old, female, male, grumpy, happy, benevolent, and angry. I

> heard them all! It stopped me in my tracks! After that moment, I felt my ability to communicate with the natural world open up. I would stop and pay attention to see if I could hear voices from the landscape.

What made this experience all the more profound was that his communication with the land came from ordinary reality. He was not under the influence of plant medicine.

"At that time, I was not in a good place creatively," Les said. "I was questioning my decision to go back to *Survivorman*. I was a bit grumpy and my creativity suffered. But this experience changed my life."

He said this experience helped him understand and trust in his ability to converse with the Earth.

> I don't even have to be immersed in nature either. I have had that same kind of deep connection in urban spaces. The Earth is always there beneath our feet! It was so intense that I actually wondered if I was schizophrenic. I went to a therapist, and she told me, "You received a gift. Go with it."

Later, while filming, Les needed some tree branches to build a shelter for the night.

"There I was with my machete glancing off the branches," he recalled. "I couldn't cut a single one! Then I stopped, caught my breath, and was like, *Man, I never asked permission*! I said, 'I am sorry. I didn't ask permission from any of you. I am taking your lives for this project. Is that okay?' And I got answers. One answered 'no.' I heeded that. And moved on to others who gave me approval. And wouldn't you know? My machete was then like a hot knife through butter. Simple, clean."

That experience helped him realize that if he didn't practice communicating with nature he could lose his line, so to speak.

> As I'm looking at the field in front of me at my home in Oregon, I feel sad for the trees. A while back, the land had been clear cut, denuded, for farming and so I planted about thirty young trees

from the nursery when we moved in. But they feel like orphans, disconnected, because they are not endemic to the area. Just transplanted orphans now. But as I say to my wife, talk to the trees. Go out and touch each one as you walk through the field and thank them for their presence.

Connection with the natural world often happens when we least expect it. Many pilgrims to Stonehenge seek and expect a sacred experience. But not Patsy. She didn't even want to be there.

> "Timelines and places merged. I felt that I was out of this world, yet wholly within it, too."
>
> —Patsy Balacchi

Stonehenge Portal

Patsy Balacchi turned fifty years old last year and decided to participate in a women's retreat that her friend Adora was hosting in the south of France. The focus of this week was on reconnecting to the energy of the Divine Feminine, specifically walking in the footsteps of Mary Magdalene, according to accounts in some of the gnostic gospels.

As popularly believed, but not yet accepted by the Roman Catholic Church, Mary Magdalene was arguably the most significant figure in Jesus's life. She was an empowered and charismatic leader, bringing Jesus's teachings to many throughout the European continent.

This pilgrimage entailed deep cleansing and the release of past pain and suffering carried throughout our lives. It was a powerful release of emotions, and she personally felt transformed by the experience.

After the retreat, Patsy accompanied her friend to London where she was doing book signings for her recently published book. But being in London, after a week of the French countryside, proved to be too stimulating for them. Adora suggested they leave the city for a brief respite and perhaps visit Stonehenge.

> To tell you the truth, I had never had Stonehenge on my bucket list. It really didn't matter to me if I saw it or not, but I agreed. It sounded like a good chance to get back to some stillness.

That morning, they took the early train out of London and two hours later, they arrived in Glastonbury. With few mass transport choices available, they rented a car to take them the final leg of their journey. Then the strangest thing occurred.

> While in the car, I started feeling palpitations, but I wasn't nervous. My heart was fluttering. They got stronger the closer we got to Stonehenge. As we got out of the car, it was very cold and windy, and the sensations in my body shifted. They felt like light punches to my stomach, essentially the solar plexus chakra [just above the belly button].

As most tourists do, they wandered around the site and got their bearings, viewing the henge from all around.

"It is so unfortunate that we were not able to walk inside the henge but we accepted our place at the periphery," Patsy recalled.

Being very spiritual, the pair couldn't leave this site without doing meditation. So Adora suggested that they do an invocation. They sat down on the grass cross-legged with the henge to their left, and the sun setting on their right.

> We were facing south, which wasn't consciously done. But as I think of it now, the shaman always faces south when conducting ritual and ceremony—the full path of the sun.

She fell into her usual meditation posture with her head upright and hands gently in her lap.

Suddenly, everything turned to light.

> I was surrounded by a column of bright white light and other pillars of light around me. I understood those pillars to be other beings surrounding me. The visuals and sensations were intense and vibrant, yet I could not hear a thing. I felt *colors* in my hands—beautiful shades of cobalt, indigo blues, and aquamarine. It was transparent, yet full of vibrant hues. My hands had rays of light beaming out from the center of my palms.

She described herself in a state of suspension and wonder.

> The feeling of awe washed over me. There were no words. Only feelings of complete peace, stillness. The sensations were odd. The colors had a feeling of cool spring water that smelled like sweet flowers. There was a tingling feeling, yet it felt hollow, as if cold air was going through my hands.

She remembered trying to see her hands, but the light obscured them as if they were no longer there.

> The light moved like ripples of water. I understood then that we are super beings full of so much potential that we haven't been able to grasp. Timelines and places merged. I felt that I was out of this world, yet wholly within it, too.

She said during the meditation she had no concept of time and couldn't tell how long this reverie lasted.

> I finally came out of it to the sound of my friend crying. She was frightened for me! She had been calling my name with no response. When I finally opened my eyes in that sitting posture at Stonehenge, it was perhaps twenty minutes later. Although I had wanted to talk, I initially could not utter a word. That lasted about an hour.

Meanwhile, her friend took her by the hand, as they circled around Stonehenge for an hour.

> She saw that I must have experienced something profound and otherworldly, and knew that I needed to ground myself. We went for a hot bowl of soup in the village to help restore my senses fully in my body. I have experienced states like this in shamanic journeying, meditations, and dreams. But never like that.

After, she realized that this experience was an initiation of some sort.

> I knew that my calling was to do something more, to step out of my comfort zone, to no longer hide, to give voice to this numinous, amazing spiritual life that is just as important as the physical one that we are so attached to. As a child, I was "out there," but somehow I suppressed it. I heard the whispers of nature spirit. I had intuitive knowing, but I didn't have the support necessary to develop those gifts. As I believe happens to many of us, our families, communities, and cultures don't know what to do with spiritual experiences, so they stuff them down and ignores their existence.

Patsy shared that until we started talking for the interview, she was not sure that she would share this story.

> I hadn't shared it with anyone since that day, but there was something in the way I felt about participating in this project. There was a voice inside me, a knowing, that said yes, I need to share this with others. We are all going through a huge energetic shift. A new reality is dawning. Some of us see it already, peeking its head into our world. But before long, others will experience this and more. The sense of deep peace, protection, and rightness with where I am... I do believe and hope that others get to experience that as well.

I'm so glad she did share this story, which she also described as a restorative experience.

Those light beings gave me a baptism of light. They restored parts of my old self that were lost as a child. They gave me energy, enthusiasm, and excitement for what comes next, like I've never felt before.

It wasn't until I interviewed Patsy again, for my podcast, that I saw a deeper meaning to the blue light she experienced. Many of the stones creating the horseshoe and outer circle at Stonehenge are known as blue stones. Their color and verticality mimic the blue pillars of light that appeared to Patsy. She experienced this other way of "seeing" beyond these physical rocks on the earth.

When I shared that with her, it deepened the meaning she had already received.

Sometimes we have experiences that we shrug off as being too fantastical, yet we have no other explanation as to what really occurred. These stories are often pushed aside and shared with few, if anyone else. We may not hear booming mountain voices or see magical light beams and luminosity, but perhaps a shapeshifting human that may do double duty as a sprite, asking us to follow in a journey of discovery. Sally shares an unusual encounter in the forests of Japan.

"I believe that nothing happens by chance."

—Sally Augustin

The Sprite Adventure

While visiting Japan on a work assignment, Sally Augustin, with a doctorate in environmental psychology, did a side trip to visit some Buddhist temple sites before returning home to the States.

In the small temple town of Nara, outside Kyoto, Sally was sitting just inside the temple as visitors passed by to worship. With a focus on how buildings impact human behavior, she was in observation mode, while also feeling quite moved by the serene scene before her.

She admired the temple architecture, roughly four hundred years old. She was immersed in this space when she was taken aback by the approach of a tiny, old Japanese woman, dressed in a nubby, Chanel-like green suit. The woman said nothing, but beckoned Sally with her finger as if to say, "come follow me."

Uncharacteristically, Sally rose and followed the woman as she headed out of the temple complex, up to a path in the nearby forest.

> It wasn't like me to follow a stranger into the woods, but the forest path was fairly open with tall pine trees, and I could see that no one was waiting in ambush. Plus, my curiosity was piqued. Where was she leading me?

Sally followed the woman far up the hill, into the conifer forest. She heard the crunch of sand and pine needles under her feet. An amazing scent of pine and soil enveloped her.

The walk entranced her with a multi-sensory experience. Then Sally heard the distant chanting of many people, until the path finally opened to a clearing. An open-air temple with dozens of people stood before her.

The old woman signaled for Sally to stay while she continued up the hill and disappeared. So, Sally sat down again, at a respectful distance to take it all in.

> It was like a scene from a movie. I thought, *Perhaps the woman felt that I must be looking for a more authentic experience like the one in this temple surrounded by nature.*
>
> There were certainly fewer people here. There was no one else present who was not worshipping. There were no tourists. The worshippers burned incense and alternately sounded gongs

and drums. And woven throughout were the sounds of nature all around.

I sat there for a really long time. I have no idea how long. But it was like...magic.

The experience was transcendent. Peaceful. Calm.

Feeling from her heart space, Sally found that setting so captivating, the way everything came together: the forest, the people, and this temple.

Sitting there observing these people in the forest made me think about how there are a lot of people whose lives are focused on things that I am not focused on. These people are living a very different existence.

I realized that there are other things in life that matter. I felt an ocean of calm that I was suddenly in sync with, one I had never noticed before.

As Sally reflects now on this experience, twenty years later, she ponders the identity of this tiny woman and her true motives. But at the same time, her inner child wonders if she was a sprite or fairy, guiding her toward this experience?

It definitely had a dreamlike quality. Plus, my behavior was quite unusual. I would not normally just follow someone that I didn't know.

In addition to feeling a deep peace, the experience has made Sally feel better about humanity. As Sally shares, "People can be 'up to' something good."

Since then, Sally has explored other sacred sites that have contributed to the awesomeness of this experience, including Lourdes in Portugal, Shinto temples, and sacred trees. These places have the ability to comfort us at a deep level. Many cultures have significant life events that are supported by these sacred sites.

> I believe that nothing happens by chance. Experiences like this cause me to wonder what is really going on around us.

Maybe you're like me and walk the beaches, picking up random rocks. I love my encounters with the sea and sand, searching for those special stones that want to come home with me.

And perhaps you've experienced something more while rock collecting. As Mark shares his journey from a hospital bed in Korea to a Long Island beach he roams every day, he shows us that even a tiny rock can open us to a revelation of the nature of reality.

> "This experience shifted everything for me!"
>
> —Mark Setton

A Little Rock with a Powerful Message

When Mark Setton was in his thirties and in a master's program in Korea, studying Korean and Chinese philosophy, he went through a profound psychological crisis. Suffering from anxiety, he was unable to speak the language well enough to communicate his issues.

Then, he suffered from a collapsed lung.

"So, there I was, for about two weeks, immobile and suffering," he said. "The only thing I could do was feel sorry for myself, and read."

Mark bought a book recommended by one of his professors, called *Neo Confucian Thought in Action: Wang Yang-Ming's Youth* by Tu Wei Ming. That book proved to be life-changing.

He read with great interest and recalls two main theories that stood out to him at the time: One was that as humans, we have an innate knowledge of the good. Deep down, we intuitively understand what is good and humane. And more than anything, we need to listen to that voice.

The other theory is called the "Unity of Self and 10,000 things." The Chinese use the poetic term "10,000 things" to represent everything in the universe.

> As I began reading it, I thought, *Holy cow*. I had some of these experiences during my childhood. I felt so different from other children. In these instances of fleeting experiences, I felt a bond between me and the others. I misunderstood it to be telepathy; being able to read minds. So around the age of eight, on the bus to school, I would set up these experiments. I would ask my friends to play a game I made up of three cards. Each card had a shape: a triangle, a circle, and a square. I would test my ability, and theirs, to guess what the other person was viewing. Eventually, I lost my friends. They thought I was nuts!

Neo-Confucian philosopher Wang Yang-Ming had similar experiences of intuitive knowing. He went through extraordinary experiences as a youth that led him to become one of the preeminent philosophers of China. These theories, or realizations, formed the foundation of his philosophy for life.

As Mark laid there, recuperating, he experienced a deep rumble in his understanding of life. Here he was, going through one of the most difficult periods of his life. Now, he was experiencing a great moment of awakening.

> I realized that this was not a coincidence. Why is it that we need to be pushed to the limits for realizations to find their way in?

Tu Wei Ming's work impacted Mark so much, not only because of the subject, but because he was so passionate about what he wrote. He wasn't just a scholar—he wrote from the heart.

> As a child, I began to realize I was different, but I didn't want to be. Those feelings of oneness with nature—connection with people and things around me—would come out of the blue. I thought it was a telepathic ability, but it had nothing to do with the intellect.

Reading about Wang, Mark was able to put his experiences into a new context. No, it wasn't telepathy he experienced. It was a feeling of oneness.

Wang used these experiences as a route to self-transformation. Rather than fleeting, unexpected moments of oneness, he realized that transformation can be the result of many years of cultivation. Rather than being accidental.

> That blew my mind. I was given glimpses of what one could experience on a more regular basis.

After living in Asia for many years, Mark came to the US to teach philosophy at the State University of New York at Stony Brook, Long Island. There, he immersed himself in the beauty of nature. Living on the North Shore, Mark slowly began to explore the coastal beaches.

> I'm a beach bum. I go to the beach probably two to three times a week, no matter what time of year it is.

One fall day, late in the afternoon, after classes, Mark took a walk on his favorite beach.

It was low tide and he was able to walk farther along this expanse of beach than usual. As he watched the long shadows of the sun low in the sky behind him, he noticed a large heart-shaped rock on the sand, apparently brought in by the last high tide earlier in the day.

> I picked it up and I remember looking at it. Then, there was like, an explosion. All at once, I was in another world. It's hard to describe. My ego seemed to dissolve. I suddenly understood Wang's description of the unity of 10,000 things. It was an awakening.

What Mark felt, he said, could be called love.

Wang Yang-Ming would say that the essence of love is unity: When barriers between self and other—be it a person or a rock—dissolve. He explains that the very essence of the Confucian concept of humanity (ren) is the feeling of oneness with animate and inanimate beings.

> I can only describe this as a feeling of love and compassion with this rock. It was like the rock was talking to me. It was saying, "You dummy! I have always been here. There's a million rocks like me. We're all like this. I just happened to be in a heart shape to wake you up!"

At this time in his life, he said he was relatively happy and peaceful. His mind wasn't filled with worry, and he was engaged with the beach and present in the moment.

> This experience shifted everything for me! It was like the proverbial butterfly flapping its wings in Mexico, which turns into a tornado in China. It's impossible to overstate the significance of this event in my life.

At the time, Mark was teaching at the University of Bridgeport in Connecticut, and he was in the process of launching a nonprofit The Pursuit of Happiness, an organization providing information about the science of well-being to high school students.

> I had the plan, but this was the kick I needed to get it rolling.

After this experience, Mark felt the power of synchronicity in a big way. He suddenly realized that when he stopped thinking about himself and turned his thoughts to how he could be of service to others—that was the key to synchronicity.

> I realized that when I'm in that zone, things happen, people call. What seemed impossible becomes possible.

Magical encounters with nature often occur when we are in a dark place. When we need to shift our perspective and witness something that cannot be explained away. We need to wake up to see our true selves, like Mark's story on the previous pages. During a workshop, my friend and teacher, Kim Hermanson mentioned this story about an owl and I realized that I needed to hear more.

> "Like we were taking this route together and we were companions on a journey. And that's when time stopped, or shifted…"
>
> —Kim Hermanson

Third Space

This was a story that Kim told many times. But this telling revealed even a deeper meaning than she realized. Sometimes that happens. We need that bigger perspective that only the passage of time and experience can bring.

There is an arc, or thread, that connects two major experiences in her life which led to and continued to feed her spiritual calling.

First, it was 2008 and Kim was teaching PhD courses at Meridian University in the Bay Area of California. During a conversation with the department head, she was asked what she wanted to teach in the upcoming session. The word "metaphor" spilled out of her mouth.

She had no idea what "metaphor" meant. At least, not in the way that it would be a viable topic for her to teach a group of PhD candidates. The department head agreed that she'd teach a course entitled "The Psychology of Metaphor."

Something happens when we follow our life purpose. We start seeing synchronicities everywhere. We are in the flow. Kim was no stranger to spiritual experiences. She had many encounters with spirit before. So she did not doubt this calling.

Not long after the course ended, Kim had another experience. What started out as a dream turned into a vivid shamanic journey.

It was a dream that was so powerful, it transformed her life path.

At first, she was in the garden at her childhood home in Iowa. But the environment in the dream wasn't normal. Everything was pulsating with color and beauty. It was numinous. Then, Kim was suddenly lifted out of the yard and pushed through the sky.

> There was this urgency. The power was so fierce and strong. It felt like I was being pummeled through the sky. When I came to a mountain range, I was sure that I was going to be pulverized, but I was suddenly swooped into a tunnel going through the mountain in a train.
>
> I looked out the windows and there was this pulsing beauty again. And then a voice said, "Third space."
>
> Nothing was the same after this. I knew the rest of my life was to teach this vision.

This dream was so dramatic and with such a sense of urgency that it was a clear wake-up call to penetrate the truth she witnessed in this dream and her role in shaping this visionary path. But filled with fear and self-doubt, she wondered, *How can I own this spiritual mission? Who am I to take this on?*

And so, four years into working toward this dream, Kim had lost all her steam. She was despairing and exhausted. Having just ended a relationship with the love of her life, and finding little success in this career path, following this vision, Kim felt like a failure on all fronts. And Kim had recently turned fifty.

It was then that she entered a self-imposed exile. A hermitage of sorts.

She moved to a small cabin on a friend's vacation property to find her bearings again in Siskiyou County. The town of Hornbrook, right off Interstate 5, consisted of a post office, a bar, and a gas station.

She thought, *This is a place I can hear myself breathe.*

The desolation of a few scrubby trees in the desert landscape mirrored the desolation of her life at that time.

She enrolled in a month-long workshop to get a better sense of her life path. But since the cell service was unreliable in this remote area, Kim drove into the big town to do the phone sessions.

During one of these sessions, the host had them break into groups of two, to have more personal discussions about the work. Kim shares, "I heard myself say that I'm a 'world teacher.' I had no idea where this notion came from! It just came out of me."

Again, these words just slipped out of her mouth.

Although Kim was no stranger to teaching, as she was currently employed by two universities for courses on psychology and other topics, she had never considered the expansiveness of the statement she just made.

That night, once the group session was over, Kim got back in her car to head home. In the dark January evening, the narrow road clung to the edges of the forest on one side and the Klamath River on the other. It was a wild and pitch-black twenty-five-minute ride home.

> I had lived there long enough to know this road well. I could anticipate the curves. But I also knew when it was time to be very focused, where a small shoulder on the right gave way to a steep drop off to the riverbank. And it was here that the owl suddenly flew right across my windshield, coming from the river.

It was close enough for Kim to see all its feathers in detail, its wings spread out took up the expanse of the windshield. A great horned owl.

> All of a sudden there was a huge bird in my windshield, so close I should have hit it. What I remember vividly is how lit up it was—I could see its stripes and feathers. The night was pitch black and I was in the middle of nowhere, so my headlights must have lit up the owl, but my memory is that it was on my windshield, not so far away as to be in front of my car, if that makes sense. The owl couldn't have gotten any closer to me—it wanted my attention.
>
> After the brush with my windshield, it flew next to me on my left, next to my driver's side window...like we were taking this route together and we were companions on a journey. And that's when time stopped, or shifted...
>
> The next thing I recall is that I found myself driving up the road to my cabin. The owl was gone. Somehow, I'd lost track of

> time... I had no memory of driving the remaining stretch of road along the river.

She completely lost herself...and her sense of time.

> I had a good fifteen minutes more of driving before I got home, and before I felt conscious again.

It was as if Kim's consciousness was suspended, somewhere else. Time stood still yet passed without her being aware of it.

According to shamanic cultures and the tradition of power animals, the owl has great spiritual meaning. It is related to wisdom, intelligence, and protection. Moreover, owls' spectacular vision and the ability to fly silently are qualities that shamans associate with great spiritual power. Owls guide those that need to see beyond the obvious, into the unseen realm.

And this is where is gets spine-tingly for me.

Kim describes Third Space as "the deep, extraordinary beauty and underworld creative energy that can't be accessed through our thinking... or ordinary means of perception." She was working with Third Space as a means of receiving guidance on one's path.

The symbol of the owl, helping others to see into the unseen realm, was quite startlingly a direct message from spirit. It was a much-needed validation of her path, urging her to continue.

And another thing that I reflected on when hearing this story: the owl she encountered flew from her right to her left. Although that doesn't sound particularly steeped with meaning, it is. The right is considered the masculine, action-taking, rational mind, whereas the left side is the feminine, the intuitive, receptive, mysterious.

The movement of the owl was a message of going within.

> Because of this encounter with the owl, I knew that this was a sign that I was not a total failure. I felt it was confirmation that I am indeed a world teacher—or would be. Those words that had just bubbled up from my subconscious that night were indeed a proclamation.

Ever since then, I teach about this channel that needs to be opened within us. We don't have that connected place in nature anymore. We go on vacation in the forest, but we don't even notice that there may be something there speaking to us.

We have to get reattuned to the natural world. There is a rich nurturing that is happening between us and the Earth, feeding our life, meaning, purpose, connectedness. It starts young.

For Kim, the owl was a much-needed confirmation to not be swayed by the trials and tribulations of our everyday lives. To know that she had a calling, a purpose to bring to life and share with others all over the world.

A week after our session about this story, Kim and I regrouped. She had just returned from a long weekend in the Bay Area, visiting some friends, and while in a second-hand shop, she turned and found a painting of owls staring at her! They now have an honored space in her home office.

And finally, the town in which she had this great horned owl encounter is called Hornbrook. I just love the synchronicities hidden within these stories, if we allow ourselves to delve deeper.

Time shifts, we receive sudden revelations, but sometimes, encounters can be extremely physical, as I experienced with this majestic pine.

> "There really was nothing like it.
> To me, it felt like coming home."
>
> —Maureen Calamia

Third Eye Wake-Up Call

Back in 2014, while up in the Adirondacks to visit our son at Paul Smith's College, we pulled into a small lot with a hiking trail. After our six-hour journey that morning, we decided to take a small walk around a pond that was surrounded by huge pine trees.

Perhaps you've experienced this before in a pine forest you've visited. If not, let me describe it. When I entered the trailhead in the Adirondacks, I was hit with an overwhelming, soul-satisfying scent of pine that enveloped my senses. There really was nothing like it. To me, it felt like coming home, which was strange, because I've never lived anywhere other than Long Island—a place not known for its pinetree forests—at least in this lifetime.

With my senses immersed in this gorgeous space, we walked slowly through the beautiful trail, admiring the trees. When I got to the other side of the pond, one tree was illuminated by the sunlight making its way through the forest canopy. It seemed to call to me and I approached it, asking permission to connect with its energy.

I softly raised my hands and hovered a few inches from the trunk and stood firmly in front of it. What happened next was stunning and completely unexpected.

I was suddenly pushed backward, as if someone had struck my forehead with the heel of their hand. It was with such force that I stumbled backward, nearly falling down. My husband, standing next to me, asked, "What happened?"

So, this is what I experienced and how I can best explain it:

I was suddenly smacked between the eyes—the area known as the third eye chakra—and saw, in my mind's eye, an image of an eye. It reminded me of the Eye of Horus, an Egyptian symbol said to represent healing and spiritual protection. And that is what happened.

At this time in my life, I was working more with trees and, in fact, was getting ready to host a workshop with two experts, Dr. Jim Conroy and Basia Alexander, who would train us on their method of connecting with and healing trees.

So, the messages that I understood from this experience were: 1) wake up and be more mindful of nature and its beings, and 2) this is what you need to do, but in your own way.

And perhaps there was a third message, which occurs to me now, as I write this passage:

Share this story with others so that they may understand the importance of their own unique ways of connection.

I have shared this story whenever I teach others about connecting with the energies of the Earth and in my earth healing workshops.

This was such a startling encounter, and I was fortunate to have a witness. I've never questioned my sanity—I didn't imagine this. It was the first time I'd ever had a "supernatural" experience that physically touched or moved my body.

My experience was one of receiving an image in my mind, which is one way of receiving messages. Sometimes I get an emotion or feeling in my body, or I hear sounds. Kara shares how she actually heard a distinct voice and had a lengthy conversation.

> "It felt completely normal at first and then the shock came afterward. *I just spoke to a tree.*"
>
> —Kara Daniels

The Grandfather Tree

Kara Daniels, an animal communicator of many years, has always felt like an advocate and voice for nature and the beings with whom we share this Earth.

She had always been deeply connected to nature and animals and knew that she was called to do something powerful in service to nature but didn't really know what that was. Over time, she tried many different career paths that did not work out. One day, she unexpectedly started communicating with a cat and that's the beginning of her story.

Kara learned how to communicate with animals energetically and telepathically, and, soon after, wonderful things started happening. She found her true calling. But a pivotal moment occurred about a year later.

> I felt really stuck in my animal communication journey. Something didn't quite feel right. While I loved connecting animals with their guardians and sharing their messages, I knew there was more to what I was supposed to do and part of me missed the wild aspect of my soul.

So, she decided to take a walk in the forest, for some mental clarity and guidance. She took her dogs and had this whole plan of what she would do on the walk.

> I was planning to hike five miles, clear my head, and get some exercise. I had my to-do list in mind, but when I got to the trail, I had a desire to just sit and connect with the trees. I felt like I was supposed to connect or communicate with the trees much like I did with animals, but I honestly had no idea what I was doing. I had heard of people that could communicate with trees but thought that to have such a connection, you'd have to be special or something. But I went with the flow with a curious mind. I set my intention that if there happened to be a tree out in the forest that wanted to connect, I was open.
>
> I walked about a quarter mile, and suddenly, a single tree magnetically called me in. This particular tree was down in a little valley below me, so it wasn't in direct line of sight of where I was walking, which made the feeling of the magnetic pull even more intriguing. I walked toward the energy, or pulling sensation, that I was feeling and just over a small hill, where I saw this beautiful tree in a meadow, right next to a creek. It looked like a great place to rest, and I had an intuitive hit that maybe this was the tree that was calling me in to connect. At this point, I wasn't ready to stop and rest so I decided that I'd check in later.

Kara took a few more steps, and then she felt a stronger tug.

> The tree was like, "Nope, right now." So, I turned around, walked to the tree, sat down and I thought, *Now what do I do? Do I just sit here?* I decided to relax and watched the water for a few moments. I then looked at the tree, really admiring its beauty and height when suddenly, I felt this almost grandfather-like presence come into my space; it felt like the tree was giving me a hug.
>
> I then heard his voice, this tree's voice, and he was so excited that somebody could hear him! I could feel his energy so strongly at this point and we ended up having the most beautiful conversation.

He shared with Kara that there's so much more than what most people can see or perceive. He said that she was currently going through a growth period and transitioning from animal communication to opening her awareness into the broader spectrum of all of nature.

> After our conversation, he dropped a pinecone on my head and told me to take the cone home with me as a reminder of our conversation. He said that I can connect with him that way across a great distance. Several years later, I still have his pinecone and I connect with him regularly for guidance or sometimes just to say hi and see how he's doing.

After they closed that conversation, Kara thought she would go finish her walk and let this experience just sink in.

> It was one of those moments where I knew that I had just had a heartfelt conversation with a tree, and it felt completely normal at first—the shock came afterward. *I just spoke to a tree. What?* It took me a minute to process what had happened.

When she continued her walk, she saw a snakeskin. But it was early spring, and the snakes really weren't out yet. The significance was not missed by Kara. Snakes are one of her animal guides and messengers. They represent transformation, shedding new skin, and growing into something new.

The symbolism was powerful!

> What was even more interesting was that, as I kept going, I saw another snakeskin. Then another one. I saw three different snakeskins within a span of three miles, and I knew that it was not a coincidence that I had just had an amazing conversation with a tree and was now spotting snakeskins, which represent transformation for me.

All of these wonderful pieces fell into place. She knew in her heart that she was on the right path. Things were shifting and coming into her awareness.

> It was such a pivotal experience for me that completely changed the direction of my life and really helped define who I am today.

The pinecone makes it all the more real for her. It helps remind her that she is not crazy. The tree was so happy that somebody recognized his presence.

> He could tell that I was questioning my role and purpose in life and was looking for direction regarding my next steps. He asked kindly to offer some guidance after explaining that he could feel my energy and understand my soul calling. He told me to continue talking with the trees and offered to be one of my acting guides. He also said that I can talk to all beings of the Earth. He then began giving me tips on how to do this and how to teach others.
>
> All across the board—not just trees, but the beings of the water and the stones—they all miss that connection with humanity. We need to bridge that connection. I feel that at this point, the trees are almost screaming to get our attention, to bring us back into relationship with nature beings.

Kara shares that over the past year, a lot more people are reaching out to her saying this also happened to them. A lot of people are spontaneously connecting or feeling a calling to forge a deeper connection to the Earth.

Maybe they were connected as children, maybe not, but now is the time to reconnect or rekindle that spark.

Kara grew up in a suburban environment with sidewalks and neighbors, but her mom was a gardener. They had a beautiful backyard with amazing flowers, birds, butterflies, and a ton of animals such as rabbits, chinchillas, birds, and dogs. She was a naturally sensitive child and tuned into the natural landscape.

Her parents loved adventure, so every summer they would go into the mountains, to camp and hike.

> It was amazing. That's where I felt like I belonged. I didn't belong in the city. I belonged out in the mountains with the moose and the bears—that's really where my soul felt alive. I remember when I was six years old, I was walking down a trail and there was a moose in front of me. I thought that it was the most amazing thing ever. I can't say that I talked to animals then, but I was overly sensitive to their feelings, or at least it felt that way. I would say I was an empathic child. I cared more than most people, and I knew on some level that there was more to the animals than what most people assumed.

When considering the snake and its role in this story, Kara shared that her mom would often bring pets home that her students didn't want anymore, one of which was a ball python.

> I loved him dearly. He was one of my best friends. He would wrap around my waist and my arms, and we would just hang out together. That was my first introduction to snakes. As I grew, I realized that they were always in my space, but the symbolism didn't really come until I started learning more about how spirit works with me and how nature communicates with us in a symbolic way. As soon as I made that connection, I realized that every time I find myself in a transitional phase or a change in my life, snakes are everywhere and really making themselves known.

Invitation: Remember

If I am right, then many of us have had experiences that we cannot explain. And for some of us, that is the reason we have never shared these stories with another. Or perhaps with just a few people with whom we can safely share.

Because these stories are rarely, if ever, retold, they can recede from active memory. But they can be recalled at the right time in our lives, to assist us to another stage of personal growth and spiritual transformation.

Did any of these stories shared here, or earlier in the book, spark a memory that may seem like an imagination gone wild? Have you ever explained away an experience because it just seemed too bizarre or wild to have happened the way you experienced it?

Has anyone ever made you feel foolish because of a story that you swear happened? Maybe your parents when you were a child?

Journal any of these memories. Do not edit your words. Allow your stories to breathe without judgement. And see what opens up for you.

CHAPTER 10

What's Your Story?

"You didn't come into this world, you came out of it like a wave from the ocean."

—Alan Watts

Throughout this book, I have shared stories from many people. From stories of a sunset providing feelings of love and relief to grieving the loss of a loved one to fantastical encounters with star beings.

I believe that many if not most of us have had profound experiences in the natural world but have either forgotten or disregarded them. Perhaps it was a moment of revelation in nature, a profound dream, or an inner knowing. Maybe it was a guided meditation in a workshop, a sunrise, or a synchronicity while having a discussion with a friend. But these events are momentary and often quickly forgotten.

Why Do We Dismiss Our Experiences?

There are several reasons why this may happen:

First, maybe we don't recognize them as significant.

We have been collectively brainwashed by religious and spiritual authorities to expect dramatic events. The drama of the burning bush and the physicality of Archangel Gabriel's visit to Mary are such examples. These stories seem to signal a verifiable, no-disputing-its-occurrence event.

Yet spiritual experiences tend to be much more subtle. They require a great deal of trust and strength to recognize them for what they are. This is, after all, about our understanding of energy and spirituality. Straightforward, linear-type occurrences are not possible in this realm of our reality.

Maybe we think that we are not enlightened enough to have them.

We may think, *Who am I? I am not worthy of this. I am not evolved enough yet.* But who are we to judge that we aren't ready?

Maybe we fear change.

If we acknowledge the event as one of a spiritual nature with profound significance, it may require us to shift our worldview. This can be scary. It can be destabilizing for many people. We often crave comfort with what is familiar. We can be uncomfortable with the prospect of the unknown. For some, it requires too much of a shift and ignoring is easier than changing their worldview so radically.

Maybe we fear being judged.

Who among us has not had moments of going along with the group even though we think differently? In our culture, most people would rather bury their stories than be perceived as a "kook." But over these last few decades, even scientists are stepping out of their comfort zone, risking their reputations and future job potential, recognizing that we haven't acknowledged the full mystical reality before us. That our reality cannot be fully known. That there are things that we can never explain. That there is consciousness and intelligence even in a drop of water!

Maybe it's because we have no framework.

Maybe one of the biggest hindrances to our acknowledgement and integration of the event was a lack of framework or guidance on how to think about it. We were no longer cared for by indigenous elders who would watch the spiritually maturing youth. These elders were there for these enchanted experiences, which were coveted and heralded as marks of spiritual awakening.

These guides would provide a safe container for discussion and assimilation.

Without a guide to acknowledge and confirm our experience, we mostly disregard these precious gifts that the Divine freely gives us. It is the brave few that hold onto our profound experience, hold them tenderly, like a butterfly in our open hands. Observing and interacting with curiosity and wonder.

There are those that seek out guidance, a mentor, or guru that can perhaps give them a context for their experience. Some seek this mentor their entire lives. There are those that express their experience of mystery in their art, their writings, their creative inspiration.

When starting to awaken to my spiritual path, I sought teachers for guidance, and still do. I have many wise elders to thank. Those that resonated truth deep within me. Some, from books, and others, during workshops and sessions. Even some who I can call dear friends. I have developed a circle, a community that has nurtured the unfoldment of my authentic self.

When we integrate these experiences, we are shifting our worldview. We are awakening.

Without integration, our experiences won't have the lasting impact they're meant to have in our lives—whether it's transforming our relationships with others, ourselves, the earth, or our life's calling.

Proof

We might decide that the only way to acknowledge this experience as real is to replicate it, in order to prove its legitimacy.

In many dreams, I have tried to photograph something. Time after time, when the camera showed up, I wondered, *What is the metaphor here that I need to understand?*

In every dream, either the camera malfunctions or photos are lost. I realized that the photograph is a metaphor for the proof some of us desire with these sacred experiences. We so desperately want proof, to show another that yes, this did happen. And maybe it's for us, too, to prove we aren't "losing it." But we can have no solid proof. We must have trust in experience.

For Mark, he has that rock that he found on the beach that transported him to a sense of oneness. For Kara, she has the pinecone that Grandfather tree dropped on her head. These are but souvenirs, that remind us of our experience, not proof.

For me, I had my husband witness me being pushed off balance, nearly falling over, when the pine tree was "waking me up." Patsy's friend witnessed her unmovable silence at Stonehenge. These are but physical symptoms for what is happening inside of us, inside of our hearts.

No camera can photograph the light we are receiving. The dialogue that is transpiring. The knowledge that is being imparted. The expansive warmth and dissolution into a sea of oneness. We are forever changed. Our consciousness is upgraded, whether we recall it or not.

Sharing

The participants in this book share experiences that they either intended to share with me prior to our discussion or shared spontaneously once the conversation seemed guided in that direction. Some participants were surprised that our conversation brought a story to the surface which had laid dormant for many years.

And because of this, I believe that a great way to integrate these amazing stories more fully into our lives is to share them with others, either through oral tradition or the written word.

One of the most valuable things we can do in spiritual communities is share our experiences. When we do, it may illuminate a formerly forgotten event for someone else. It may stir up memories that were ignored.

So often, when people start sharing, others will say they had a similar experience and dismissed it as fantasy. Sometimes, people in the group will share a similar symbol or metaphor and that will help them both acknowledge its significance.

And what is most important, is that we alter our perspective and open our minds to these messages from nature, from the sacred source. And when we open up, we allow more connections and experiences in.

To illustrate this point, I will share another story of how the deer symbol, which appeared in a dream nearly twenty years ago, has become a significant guide for my life's path, through both dreams and waking life.

Themes Weaving Over Time

I do a lot of journaling, and I highly recommend it as a regular practice. Why? Because timing is everything, and we can see more at the fifty-thousand-foot view.

When I read through past journals, I often notice recurring themes that have appeared at key moments in my life. I've also discovered significant symbols that have guided me in pursuing my life's purpose. And one of them, for me, is deer, and specifically, Charlotte.

First, I had what I titled my "Deer Dream" and I had no idea what it meant at the time, but I immediately trusted that its message would somehow steer me along my career path.

Early in the 2000s, I was at a turning point in my life. I was going through a spiritual awakening and knew that I must pursue a different career related to my spiritual work. But I did not know what was next. Impatiently, I waited for a sign. It came to me in the form of a dream a few months later, the very day that I was laid off from my ten-year position at a marketing firm.

In short, the dream was about violence against deer in New York City. And somehow, I told the mayor that we needed to plant trees to reduce violence. And although I have never been a person connected with angels, there was an angel present, that only I saw, during my meeting with the mayor.

I call this my "Deer Dream" and when I awoke, I had no idea what it meant but I trusted that it had something to do with a new career path. Its significance and guidance have unfolded slowly ever since, first in my decision to do feng shui training, then in learning about biophilic design, and in rituals and ceremonies to heal the Earth.

A few years ago, during a course in ecopsychology, I suddenly realized the significance of the name of my hometown of Deer Park and connection with the Buddha, who was enlightened in the "Deer Park." And my connection with Buddhism and the form of feng shui that I practice, which is immersed with Buddhist practices and rituals.

Ever since, my work is dedicated to helping others build a relationship with the Earth and co-create with it, which is the essence of this book.

So, what about Charlotte? Oh, she's a beauty.

When I started working on getting support for this book, back in November 2020, I was at an outdoor yoga class at the nature center where I volunteer. Charlotte is a resident doe who loves being around humans. She may even think that she is one!

This November morning, because of Covid restrictions, we met outside for class in a rather brisk forty-five degrees. I wore a pair of wool socks throughout the class. As often happens, Charlotte visited us during our asanas. She walks around, sniffs, and sometimes licks us. She is very sweet.

But something completely out of character happened that morning.

She hung around me, stepped onto my mat, and while I went into side angle, an inverted posture, she jumped up and placed her front hooves on my back. In the turmoil of me shouting and jumping up, she stepped on the side of my foot—and thankfully I was wearing those heavy wool socks!

The rest of that fall and winter, we did yoga via Zoom, and when the early-morning weather was finally warm enough, in mid-May, we rejoined outside on the lawn at the center.

And Charlotte came around again to join us, while we recounted what had transpired just six months ago.

Maybe she heard us because she jumped on me again (which never happened to anyone before or since).

She was pregnant, and, just a few days later, she gave birth to two fawns.

I realized that the interval between these two experiences—a deer's typical gestation being six months—spanned from the beginning to the end of her pregnancy, metaphorically giving me the green light from Mother Earth that this book would be completed. And indeed, it was fully written in six months.

So in this way, journaling has been an invaluable tool to see the arc of my storyline. I journal sacred experiences.

When I journal about an experience, I am sure to date the event so that I can look back and make these connections between events and across time. I enter posts in my dream journal, as both waking and dreaming life can provide significant information from nature to help guide our lives.

I have written about and retold my Deer Dream before. But when writing this book, I went back to reread my entry and it was only then that I realized, to my astonishment, that it was the same day that I was laid off from my job, and I had been actively seeking guidance on a new path. The date was critical to my understanding of the full meaning of the message.

And I continue to watch for deer, as confirmation of—or a divergence from—my path.

What Are Your Stories?

Hey, it's time we turned our attention to you. Yes, you.

Here we are, at the end of this book, where you read lots of stories of amazing nature connections. And I am hoping that, in between reading, when you put the book down at night, you were thinking about your own.

Perhaps you have new context for some of your experiences. Perhaps you have stories that are like some shared in this book.

If I called you right now, and asked, "What is your story?" what would be the first one that comes to mind? Or rather, what story arises from your heart?

Maybe you are thinking that your story isn't magical enough. Or, that you probably misremembered it and it really didn't happen that way. Or, you may have never told another soul about it. Or maybe this story surfaced while reading this book and you owe it some time to contemplate the deeper meaning and heartfelt experience of it.

I do hope that stories are pouring out of you. I do hope that you decide to journal them, either handwritten or digital. If you're not a writer, then do a voice recording for documentation.

When stories resurface later in our lives, there is usually a connection between the life situations in these time periods. There is something that wants to be acknowledged. Consider the symbols and metaphors for what occurred. Always consider first your personal meanings for symbols, then you may decide to consult a reference book or website to flesh out a richer meaning with your life.

If you had an experience and are dismissing the magical aspects as your imagination, consider why you remember the experience this way. Maybe it did actually happen, as with Sally's sprite story (Chapter 9).

What were the messages you gained? How did the experience impact your life, or perhaps how was it meant to impact it? If you are having trouble with the more fantastical connections, just tell the story as if it were a dream, or a folktale. See how that feels.

Consider sharing with others. They may surprise you by sharing a story of their own!

In these last few years, more people have been awakening. And more people are looking for guidance and support from those "elders" that will help them to frame their experiences. To integrate these stories into their own personal mythology and follow their life's purpose.

Gather New Stories

Hopefully you have spent some time thinking about your past. But what about now?

Often, our experiences are spontaneous, unplanned. A flock of birds fly overhead just as you were wondering if you and your family should move. You find a calming, peaceful place to sit in the woods, just when you need it the most. A thunderstorm makes you pause on a stressful day, and you are filled with awe and mystery.

And sometimes, we may want to seek out a connection to nature. Just don't expect anything to happen. But, as the exercises in this book demonstrate, be open, be playful, be curious, like a child. Often, nature speaks in very subtle ways. Sometimes in ways that most people would not even notice.

Sometimes, if we are alert, we may notice a tug to turn down a path or street. There may be a portal opening for you.

Where Do We Go Now?

> "The world was whole then, the sun and moon together as one."
>
> —Bianca Viola

Many people have awakened to the fact that we need nature in our lives. Just as nature needs us. Ironic that. Given all the grief we have dished out over the centuries.

It is my hope that this book has spurred you to be more mindful of the importance of nature in your life and make it a priority to engage in nature connection for your health and well-being in body, mind, *and spirit*.

Perhaps you will share this book with others.

Perhaps you will contribute to this work in the future. Or you will be inspired to do something else that will help others to connect with nature. (There are resources at the end of this chapter for further information.)

Let me end with this story from just the other day.

I witnessed the 2024 Total Solar Eclipse. We weren't assured, after all that travel, that we would actually see it due to weather conditions, but we did. And let me tell you, it is worth it.

Now I know why people are Eclipse Chasers.

We traveled up to Willsboro, New York, which is a tiny hamlet in the Adirondacks adjacent to Lake Champlain. I had been there before and there is nothing there. That is why I wanted to go there.

My son's friend has a cabin on a pond. No Wi-Fi. No running water. Primitive.

But there was a bonfire, kayaks, plenty of food, and love.

A small group of us met for a few hours, starting at eleven in the morning. The eclipse started at two o'clock in the afternoon and was total at three fifteen.

We watched with mouths agape, remarking on how even when there was a tiny sliver of sun, it seemed to light up the entire landscape. But then someone turned the light off. And we spent the next three minutes and some odd seconds in complete darkness.

It was sudden and shocking. Even though I had seen it before in videos, there is no comparison to witnessing it yourself.

It brought up all sorts of thoughts about how small and insignificant we are as humans. How we think we control the world, but we really are just ants.

Our human reaction to the sudden loss of light is so visceral. Even though I understood intellectually what was happening, my heart was still in shock. The light vanished, just like that!

We could see the stars and what looked like pre-dawn light on the horizon. We heard robin calls as if it were dawn.

The hush of talk around us as we all took it in.

Then, suddenly, someone turned on the light switch, and that sliver of sun reappeared on the other side, ever so slightly from behind the moon. And everything was awash in light!

When you witness an event like this, there's a sense of belonging to something greater. Immanence is a term that I learned from my friend and contributor, Sophia Batalha. I've typically used the word "transcendence" to recall these experiences, but that evokes the idea that we rise above and step outside of our human experience.

But the idea of immanence is that we are wholly within it. Within it all. And it is moments like this that overwhelm our minds and hearts. And we crave experiencing that again.

And we know that we cannot have that immersive feeling of belonging until we pass on into the embrace of all that is. We can only experience glimpses.

I hope that as you finish this book, you come to recognize the immanence that connects us all. We are here to experience that unity in our everyday lives. On the way to the grocery store. Walking the dog. Cooking dinner. Answering a text. Talking with a friend.

In Closing

As we conclude this book, filled with tender and startling experiences, I'd like to leave you with a few final, precious thoughts.

No Pressure to Remember

Throughout this book, I have hoped that these stories would spark remembrance of your own stories. But you may have forgotten them. Like my experience at the Fairy Pool in Skye.

I cannot believe that I needed someone to prod me to remember only a few weeks later. And what's even more ironic is that I had been immersed in these sacred experiences for the past several years. And I still needed support to remember.

And what happens when we don't have an "elder" to prod us? Or what about the many people who aren't as aware of their connection to wild nature?

I brought this up after a podcast interview with an astronomer/astrologer friend of mine, Gemini Brett, and he said something I hadn't thought about: "It doesn't matter if you remember, it's still within you."

Those words rang so true to me. Do not get frustrated if you don't recall anything. Those experiences are within you and are working their magic.

When You Do Remember, Write It Down

When you recall your stories, please write them down. You will appreciate the chronicling of your experiences to aid in future reflection and discovery. There is so much richness in just one experience. When you write, take time going through the details as well as the overall impressions of the encounter.

Write about the experience from all your senses. Recall where in your body you felt it, and perhaps, still hold it. Use the invitations in this book to explore and uncover deeper meaning in your life. What are the messages that want to be known? Is there anything now in your life that is specifically enriched by the meaning of this story?

Normalize These Stories by Sharing with Others

"Normalize" is a word that we hear a lot lately. But it's interesting that the definition of "normalize" is about bringing things back to a previous state.

But when used in the context of this book, it is about bringing things up to meet a higher state, a higher consciousness. We make these enchanted, sacred, amazing encounters a part of regular human experience. I think many would agree that humanity, in its early stages, was probably more in tune with mystery, long before scientific research was thought to give us all the answers.

We must now be willing to bridge the gap between scientific knowledge and the ultimate mystery of reality.

Share your stories with others. And be available for others to share their own. There is such power to this process of remembering our enchanted experiences.

Is the "Earth Shutting Down" as My Teacher Proposed a Few Years Ago?

Well, that statement certainly got my attention. But as I stand here, now, I say, no! The trees tell me no. My dreams tell me no. Yes, we are in a great turning of humanity and consciousness. We are there right now. But we are turning toward our kinship with the natural world.

Dr. David Hawkins, in his book *Power Vs. Force: The Hidden Determinants of Human Behavior*, shared that we do not need a majority of humanity to think a certain way for change to occur. A small percentage of people is all that is needed. And I do believe we are reaching that tipping point in the near future.

And Finally, It Is Simpler Than We Think

I want to leave you with these words. "It is simpler than we think."

We tend to make things more complex than they need to be. We may feel overwhelmed by the complexities of this modern society and our personal lives.

One thing that has opened me up to greater joy is the understanding that it is simpler than we think for change to occur, for dreams to come true. We manifest our reality. We are co-creators of our lives. Everything is energy, and energy is fluid and ever-changing.

Shifting our perspective shifts our reality. It is simpler than we think.

Why do I think this way? Why do I believe, since I was twelve years old, that this picture of a bleak apocalyptic future is not my future? Some might call me an incurable optimist. But I know that I am a seer and a co-creator. And I have more power than I was being led to believe. How about you? Where are these wild, enchanted places within you?

✦ ★ ✦

I sincerely hope that you not only enjoyed this book, but that it gave you inspiration and the understanding that we are one with the natural world. Our stories can re-enchant this connection that we lost so long ago.

Go on nature therapy walks, visit parks, and spend time outside, even just outside your front door. Nature is a powerful healer and remedy for our stressful lives. Counterbalance your time on technology with nature.

If you have children, bring them into the outdoors with a joyful curiosity. Let their natural playfulness infect you. Remember, their love of nature can be nourished by a loving adult that can foster these experiences.

Journal about your experiences. It's amazing what you'll uncover weeks, months, even years later.

There are so many wonderful organizations and websites that can help you, in whatever direction you find yourself guided.

Please consider checking out my podcast, *The Enchanted Earth Podcast with Maureen Calamia*, available on YouTube, Apple Podcasts, and Spotify. In this podcast series, you'll see some of the people featured in this book as well as other amazing people wanting to share their experiences in the hopes of inspiring others.

You can also join the Facebook Group "The Enchanted Earth." In there, you will find opportunities to connect with other like-minded spirits.

And I would love to connect with you directly! I'd love to hear what this book is bringing up for you personally. How is it contributing to your exploration of your wild, authentic, and enchanted soul? How are your encounters with nature inspiring you? What are you discovering about your personal mythology? Feel free to reach out to me at maureen@luminous-spaces.com—I look forward to hearing from you!

I also offer private and group sessions to explore and share our sacred stories. You can find more information on my website: www.luminous-spaces.com.

And if you enjoyed this book, please share with others and post a review online. This is a growing movement and I do hope you will join in!

Appendix

Contributor Bios

Amanda "Pua" Walsh, MS, is the CEO and founder of Astrology Hub. She hosts the weekly *Astrology Hub Podcast*, a top-ranking astrology podcast with over 80,000 downloads per month, featuring conversations with the best astrologers in the world today. Prior to this, Amanda was a co-owner of a successful technology consulting company in New York City with a master's degree in psychology from the University of California, Santa Barbara. She left NYC and her career to embark on a more heart-centered life in Hawaii nine years ago. In her work, Amanda blends her diverse background in business leadership, psychology, digital marketing, and media with her passion for astrology, spirituality, and personal growth.

Amos Clifford is the founder of the Association of Nature and Forest Therapy Guides and Programs and author of the bestselling book *Your Guide to Forest Bathing* (Conari Press 2018). A student of Buddhist philosophy for over twenty years, Amos founded Sky Creek Dharma Center in Chico, California, where he emphasizes the importance of meditation practice in wild places. Amos is also widely known for his work in restorative justice. He is founder of the Center for Restorative Process, where they work to answer the question as to how the principles of restorative justice can inform ways to heal the broken relationships between humans and the more-than-human world of nature. Amos holds a BS in Organization Development and an MA in Counseling from the

University of San Francisco. Amos has been the primary developer of ANFT's acclaimed training programs.

Betsy Perluss (she/her), PhD, grew up as a semi-feral child on Pimu (Catalina Island), where she was ignited with a passion for wild and unbounded places. She stumbled upon the School of Lost Borders in 1998 and since has been involved as a participant, guide, trainer, board member, and member of the Elders and Guiding Councils. Betsy aspires to live a life informed by the wisdom of the land, pan-cultural ceremonies, and the mystery of initiatory rites. She is also a psychotherapist with a background in eco and depth psychology, and from 2001–2012, she was professor of counseling at California State University, Los Angeles.

Bonnie Casamassima is a researcher, educator, and highly sensitive intuitive empath. She's the founder of Intuitive by Nature, an organization dedicated to nurturing people's joy-driven lives through fostering their intuitive connections. She is a former professor holding her MFA from Savannah College of Art and Design focusing on environmental psychology and biophilic design, and a BS in interior design from the University of Tennessee at Knoxville. She lives in Knoxville, TN, with her partner and his two incredible kids. She enjoys traveling, pottery, dancing to live-music while wearing costumes, and a good belly laugh.

Craig Chalquist, PhD, is the academic program director of consciousness, psychology, and transformation at National University. His most recent book is the second edition of *Terrapsychological Inquiry: Restoring Our Relationship to Nature, Place, and Planet* (2024).

Faith Adiele writes and speaks about race, culture, and travel. She is author of *Meeting Faith*, a memoir about being ordained as Thailand's first Black Buddhist nun which won the PEN Open Book Award and routinely appears on travel listicles. Her media credits include Sleep Stories (*CALM* app), two episodes of *A World of Calm* (HBOMax), and the documentary *My Journey Home* (PBS) about finding her family in Nigeria. Founder of the nation's first writing workshop for travelers of color, she teaches at California College of the Arts and leads writing workshops around the world. Follow her at adiele.com and @meetingfaith.

Gordon Hempton, acoustic ecologist, has circled the globe three times in pursuit of the Earth's rarest sounds. His sound portraits, which record quickly vanishing natural soundscapes, have been featured in *People* magazine and a national PBS television documentary, *Vanishing Dawn Chorus*, which earned him an Emmy. Hempton provides professional audio services to media producers, including Microsoft, the Smithsonian, National Geographic, and the Discovery Channel. Recipient of awards from the National Endowment for the Arts and the Rolex Awards for Enterprise, he is the coauthor of *One Square Inch of Silence: One Man's Quest to Preserve Quiet* (Free Press/Simon & Schuster, 2010) and a founding partner of Quiet Parks International. Gordon Hempton speaks widely about the importance of listening.

Hobie Hare helps people connect with nature through guided tours of national parks and other protected wild places, photography, speaking, and mentoring. Hobie worked as a Yellowstone National Park ranger for eight seasons, including one winter at Fishing Bridge near Yellowstone Lake. He also worked as a Yellowstone Forever Institute instructor and naturalist guide for six seasons. As an international and outdoor educator prior to working in Yellowstone, Hobie taught English as a Second Language and first-year seminar courses at Montana State University and has also lived and worked in Costa Rica, Thailand, Japan, Venezuela, and Australia.

Itzhak Beery is an acclaimed author and internationally respected shamanic teacher, healer, speaker, and trip leader. Raised in an Israeli Kibbutz, he had a fine art career and owned an ad agency in NYC; a midlife crisis led him from a set skeptic into a dedicated spiritual seeker. Since 1995, he has integrated the teachings from his indigenous and Western teachers. He was initiated into the "Circle of 24 Yachaks of Imbabura" in Ecuador and with the Amazonian Kanamari Pajè in

Brazil. Beery founded ShamanPortal.org, the Andes Summit, and *SPQR* magazine and cofounded the New York Shamanic Circle and Amaroo Sanctuary in Mindo, Ecuador. He received the Ambassador for Peace Award from the Universal Peace Federation and the UN.

Janine Bendicksen is a dedicated wildlife enthusiast who has served as the director of wildlife rehabilitation at Sweetbriar Nature Center for the past twenty-three years. With a passion for animal welfare and conservation, Janine has played a vital role in rehabilitating and caring for a wide range of wildlife species. Her expertise and commitment to the well-being of animals have made her a respected figure in the field. Janine's work at Sweetbriar Nature Center has positively impacted countless animals and inspired others to join in the mission of protecting and preserving wildlife for future generations.

Janine Benyus is the cofounder of Biomimicry 3.8 and the Biomimicry Institute. She is a biologist, innovation consultant, and author of six books, including *Biomimicry: Innovation Inspired by Nature*. Since the book's 1997 release, Janine's work as a global thought leader has evolved the practice of biomimicry from a meme to a movement, inspiring clients and innovators around the world to learn from the genius of nature. Clients include Ford, Boeing, Google, Microsoft, Jacobs, Levi's, and General Mills. Learn more at Biomimicry.net, AskNature.org, and the Biomimicry Center at Arizona State University.

Jean Shinoda Bolen, MD, is a psychiatrist, Jungian analyst, diplomat on the American Board of Psychiatry and Neurology, former professor of psychiatry, and an internationally known author and speaker. She is a Distinguished Life Fellow of the American Psychiatric Association and a recipient of the Institute for Health and Healing's Pioneers in Art, Science, and the Soul of Healing Award. The Association for the Study of Women and Mythology presented her the Demeter Award for her lifetime achievement in women's spirituality. Dr. Bolen has authored over ten books with over a hundred foreign editions. Her book inspired

The Millionth Circle Initiative (www.millonthcircle.org) and led to her involvement at the UN. She currently maintains a private practice in Mill Valley, California.

John "JK" Kiesendahl is the eldest son of Harry and Mary and is a managing partner of Woodloch. He attended Cornell University's School of Hotel Administration and joined the navy before deciding to make Woodloch his career. He is best known for greeting guests personally during meals and wearing the "funny" pants (he has custom-tailored pants featuring many different children's characters). He continues to provide the company with leadership and enthusiasm every day. John serves on the board of directors for the Dime Bank and is an active member of the Wallenpaupack School Board. His wife, Patti, is also very active within Woodloch and is responsible for the Woodloch Gift Shops and decorating around the resort. Together, they have seven children: Bob, Matt, Brad, Brooke, Megan, Patrick, and Olivia and are proud to say that five of them are active within the organization.

John Perkins focuses on transformation—personal, communal, and global. A leading authority on shamanism, he learned about the power of using perceived reality to change objective reality from shamans in the Amazon who saved his life—and then with other shamans on five continents. He has used shamanic practices to help individuals, corporations, universities, and governments. His eleven books, including the two latest, *Confessions of an Economic Hit Man, 3rd Edition: China's Economic Hit Man Strategy and Ways to Stop the Global Takeover* and *Touching the Jaguar*, have sold more than two million copies. In addition to his groundbreaking books on global intrigue, he has authored five books on indigenous cultures and transformation, including *Shapeshifting*. He is a founder of Dream Change and, along with Bill and Lynne Twist, the Pachamama Alliance, nonprofits dedicated to creating a regenerative, peaceful, and thriving world. He was awarded the Lennon Ono Grant for Peace, 2012—along with Lady Gaga and Pussy Riot.

Joshua Heath is an environmental education specialist at Promised Land State Park in Pennsylvania. A former outdoor adventure manager and naturalist at The Lodge at Woodloch in Hawley, PA, Josh studied Park Management at Unity College in Maine. He was certified as a forest therapy guide by the Association of Nature & Forest Therapy in 2015.

Julia Oliansky, née Plevin, is the author of *The Healing Magic of Forest Bathing* and founder of the Forest Bathing Club. Since 2015, she has been guiding individuals, groups, and organizations through healing experiences in nature. With over a decade of experience in brand and innovation strategy, she is also the founder of Heal Yourself People Earth (HYPE)—a climate creative agency for those who are ready to put the planet at the center of their purpose. Julia has a BA from Dartmouth College, an MFA from their School of Visual Arts, and training in numerous healing modalities. She lives in Ashland, Oregon.

Kara Daniels is the founder of Deep Root Connections, a place where earth, animals, nature, and spirit are all intertwined, alive and communicating. Kara is an interspecies communicator, channel for nature spirits, land healer, and teacher.

Kim Hermanson is a pioneering educator and faculty at Pacifica Graduate Institute. She has written three books on the power of the creative and "third space"—the non-cognitive visionary space that lies beyond our thinking mind: *Deep Knowing*, which won a 2022 National Indie Excellence Award; *Sky's the Limit*, which received an Independent Publisher Book Award; and *Getting Messy*. She is known for her ability to quickly shift a person out of his or her thinking mind into an intelligent field of profound beauty that lies beyond thought. Her seminars attract visionaries, pioneers, and trailblazers who are "pushing the wall" with her to bring forth a new world.

Les Stroud is credited as the creator of the survival TV genre through his groundbreaking series *Survivorman*. He's an award-winning film producer with over 160 documentaries, an author of four bestselling books, as well as a celebrated singer-songwriter known for his prowess on the harmonica. Along with thirty-one Canadian Screen Award nominations and three wins, his new children's book *Wild Outside* won the National Best Non-Fiction (Yellow Cedar Award) and the Best National Informational Book award, and is nominated for a Rocky Mountain Book Award. He has also been nominated for Best Artist and Best Group by the International Acoustic Music Awards. In 2022, he was named Canada's Chief Scout.

Lisa Kahn is the visionary behind Finding Sanctuary—the multidisciplinary design firm at the heart of the revolution of well-being in interior design. Her work is synonymous with sanctuary, epitomizing luxury, tranquility, and intentional living. Lisa leads her design team and lives with her husband and two English Springer Spaniels in Naples, Florida.

Llyn "Cedar" Roberts, MA, is an award-winning author and a celebrated teacher of healing and shamanism. Her books include *Walking Through Darkness* and *Speaking with Nature*, coauthored with Sandra Ingerman; *Shamanic Reiki*, coauthored with Robert Levy; *Shapeshifting into Higher Consciousness*; and *The Good Remembering*. Llyn is the founder of the Olympic Mountain EarthWisdom Circle (eOMEC.org), a nonprofit organization dedicated to inspiring a sacred and responsible relationship with the Earth and to preserving the ancient wisdom of indigenous peoples. She is the founder of Shamanic Reiki Worldwide, which teaches people how to heal themselves and others with nature's spiritual energy.

Maia Toll, after pursuing an undergraduate degree at the University of Michigan and a master's at New York University, apprenticed with a traditional healer in Ireland, where she spent extensive time studying the growing cycles of plants, the alchemy of medicine-making, and the psychospiritual aspects of healing. Maia maps new pathways for seeing our lives, inspiring those who encounter her work to live with more purpose, more intention, more meaning, and, maybe, even more magic. She is the co-owner of the retail store Herbiary, with locations in Philadelphia, PA, and Asheville, NC, where she lives with her partner and three ridiculously spoiled dogs. Keep up with Maia's writing on her Substack, *Unkempt*.

Mark Setton, DPhil, is the cofounder and CEO of Pursuit of Happiness. He has studied and published works on East Asian philosophy and well-being for the past thirty years. He earned his BA and MA at Sungkyunkwan University in Seoul and his doctorate at Oxford University. He has taught at the State University of New York at Stony Brook, the University of California at Berkeley, Oxford University, and, presently, the University of Bridgeport. Mark and his team design and teach educational programs on the science and implementation of well-being for secondary schools, universities, and corporations, such as Google, Mediamax, the China Accelerator, Dartmouth College, etc. He is especially interested in recent scientific discoveries on well-being, as well as the remarkable resonance between modern science and ancient wisdom.

Nicole Craanen is the founder and driving force behind the Biophilic Design Institute. She embodies her commitment to transform our relationship with our environment, guiding architects and designers to integrate our innate connection with nature directly into the core principles of design. Her influential role on key advisory boards and her journey as a yoga instructor and nature & forest therapy guide informs a philosophy that promotes health and well-being, while also working to mitigate the human impact on the non-human world. Her approach emphasizes curiosity, deep listening, and collaboration.

Nina Simons is cofounder and chief relationship officer at Bioneers and leads its Everywoman's Leadership program. Throughout her career spanning the nonprofit, social entrepreneurship, corporate, and philanthropic sectors, Nina has worked with nearly a thousand diverse female leaders across disciplines, race, class, age, and orientation to create conditions for mutual learning, trust, and leadership development.

She co-edited *Moonrise: The Power of Women Leading from the Heart*, and authored *Nature, Culture, and the Sacred: A Woman Listens for Leadership*—which includes an accompanying discussion guide and embodied practices. The book won Gold Nautilus awards in women, intersectionality, and social justice.

Oliver Heath is an architectural and interior designer, and his practice, Oliver Heath Design, is focused on delivering health and well-being in the built environment. As writers, thought leaders, and designer practitioners, they are recognized global experts in Biophilic Design (enhancing human nature connections). Oliver's media activity over the last twenty-four years has given him extensive presentation experience working for a number of television channels, including BBC, ITV, Channel 4, and the National Geographic channel. He is a passionate advocate of sustainable design and has acted as a spokesperson for the likes of the UK's Department for Energy and Climate Change (DECC), the Energy Saving Trust (EST), and the Waste and Resources Action Programme (WRAP). Design clients include the likes of Schneider Electric, Apple, Bloomberg, The BRE, Booking.com, Interface, and the John Lewis Partnership.

Patsy Balacchi is the founder, brand consultant, and feng shui expert at Zenotica, a multidisciplinary graphic design and holistic platform based in Houston, TX. Known for her dynamic and harmonious visual brands, Patsy's work provides the ideal platform for personal and professional spatial transformation.

Pete Nelson fell in love with treehouses as a child after building a backyard tree fort with his dad at their home in New Jersey. Today, he has created hundreds of treehouses around the world with his design and construction firm, Nelson Treehouse and Supply. Pete has also published six books on the art and science of treehouse-building, most recently *Be in a Treehouse*. He has also shared many of his constructed houses with global audiences as the star of the hit Animal Planet television series *Treehouse Masters*. In all of these projects, Pete has endeavored to equip others with the information and inspiration to get out into nature and up in the trees in a safe, sustainable, and fun way.

Sally Augustin, PhD, is a practicing environmental psychologist and a founder of the Space Doctors. She has extensive experience integrating neuroscience-based insights to develop recommendations for the design of places, objects, and services that support desired cognitive, emotional, and physical outcomes/experiences. Her client base is worldwide and includes organizations and individuals that produce and/or use designed solutions. Augustin, who is a fellow in the American Psychological Association, is the editor of *Research Design Connections*. Dr. Augustin is the author of *Designology* (Mango, 2019).

Sandra Ingerman, MA, is an award-winning author of twelve books, including *Soul Retrieval: Mending the Fragmented Self, Medicine for the Earth, Walking in Light,* and *The Book of Ceremony: Shamanic Wisdom for Invoking the Sacred in Everyday Life.* She is the presenter of eight audio programs produced by Sounds True. Sandra is a world-renowned teacher of shamanism and has been teaching for close to forty years. She has taught workshops internationally on shamanic journeying, healing, and reversing environmental pollution using spiritual methods. Sandra is recognized for bridging ancient cross-cultural healing methods into our modern culture, addressing the needs of our times.

Sofia Batalha is a creator, teacher, and consultant of symbolic, lunar, and feminine feng shui methods since 2003. She believes in the practice of consciously living, which depends on a strong and personal relationship with the house and with the inner world of each inhabitant. Permaculture and the birth of her first daughter opened her to the power of the sacred feminine and connection to live meaningfully with nature, as well as the importance of dignifying the power of the feminine body and honoring its cycles. She focuses on ecopsychology, transpersonal psychology and liberation, listening and radical presence, as well as ecstasy and ancient sacred connection.

Sonja Bochart connects more than twenty-five years of interior architecture experience with a concentration in healthcare project work and expertise in biophilia and regenerative design. Following work with the International Living Future Institute and an early focus on biophilic design integration, Sonja pursued her master's degree in regenerative design. Today, her work with clients intersects at the health and wellness of people and the planet. Sonja's unique approach to regenerative design thinking brings a process-oriented lens to many points—whether that occurs before the design process in order to facilitate participatory visioning and planning, throughout to manage change, or after completion to measure design impact.

Sumita Singha is an award-winning architect, teacher, and writer. She has served on many committees of the Royal Institute of British Architects, or RIBA, for over twenty-five years and on the NHS Board for nine years. Sumita is currently the RIBA Board Trustee for Education. She founded Architects For Change, the Equality forum at RIBA. Sumita is a trustee of three built environment charities and the founding director of Charushila, an environmental design charity. She has taught architecture for over twenty-five years and is the author of many publications on architecture. Sumita received an OBE for services to architecture in 2021.

Sylvie Rokab is a certified mindfulness teacher, nature-therapy guide, and an Emmy-nominated filmmaker. By blending these disciplines, Sylvie offers powerful techniques that help participants find freedom from suffering through access to the healing, wisdom, and wonder that can only be found with nature. Narrated by Liam Neeson, her film *Love Thy Nature* earned twenty-seven awards and has helped viewers realize that the delusion of disconnection from the natural world is the root cause of our dire human and ecological condition. Through her teachings, Sylvie helps participants rekindle loving awareness and awaken to the power of nature to help transform their lives—as well as to their own power to heal and regenerate our world. They often share that they take home a renewed sense of belonging, joy, aliveness, and a desire to protect our spellbinding world.

Vanessa Champion, former academic turned London newspaper editor, is editor of *The Journal of Biophilic Design*, an international podcast series on iTunes, Amazon Music, Spotify, YouTube, etc. Through insightful interviews and research with thought-leaders and activators of biophilic design, we aim to help you learn more about the positive and transformational impact biophilic design can have—not only on your city, homes, workplaces, and healthcare spaces, but also on your health and focus, your personal happiness and wellbeing, and your company's bottom line. www.journalofbiophilicdesign.com.

Contributor Contact Information

Amanda Pua Walsh	astrologyhub.com
Amos Clifford	www.natureandforesttherapy.org
Betsy Perluss	betsyperluss.com
Bonnie Casamassima	www.interweavepeopleplace.com
Craig Chalquist	www.chalquist.com
Faith Adiele	www.adiele.com
Gordon Hempton	www.soundtracker.com
Hobie Hare	yourlifenature.com
Itzhak Beery	ibeery.weebly.com
Janine Bendickson	www.instagram.com/sweetbriarnaturecenter
Janine Benyus	biomimicry.org
Jean Shinoda Bolen	www.jeanbolen.com
John Kiesendahl	www.thelodgeatwoodloch.com
John Perkins	johnperkins.org
Josh Heath	www.facebook.com/groups/774369066523842
Julie Plevin	juliaplevin.com
Kara Daniels	www.deeprootconnections.com
Kim Hermanson	www.kimhermanson.com
Les Stroud	www.lesstroud.ca
Lisa Kahn	www.lisakahndesigns.com
Llyn Roberts	www.facebook.com/llyn.roberts

Maia Toll	maiatoll.com
Mark Setton	www.pursuit-of-happiness.org
Nicole Craanen	www.rootedinnature.org/services
Nina Simons	www.ninasimons.com
Oliver Heath	www.oliverheath.com
Patsy Balacchi	zenotica.com
Pete Nelson	nelsontreehouse.com
Sally Augustin	designwithscience.com
Sandra Ingerman	www.sandraingerman.com
Sofia Batalha	www.sofiabatalha.com
Sonja Bochart	www.sonjabochart.com
Sumita Singha	www.ecologicarchitects.com
Sylvie Rokab	sylvierokab.com
Vanessa Champion	vanessachampion.co.uk

Acknowledgments

After spending a year getting rejected by celebrity agents, Pam Grout, the prolific and bestselling author of *E-Squared*, was my first "yes" to be interviewed for this book. Although her story ultimately did not make it into the book—being an experience at the Taj Mahal and not in "nature"—Pam's yes gave me the much-needed confidence to continue the project. In fact, her "yes" apparently opened the energetic floodgates for others! Within four months, this book was almost entirely written!

I want to thank my friend and colleague, Susan Chu, whose question under the oak of "What's next?" spurred this project.

This book would not have been possible without the generous sharing of stories. During my three years of working on this project, I amassed stories that would fill nearly two volumes. And regrettably, when it came time for publishing, there were necessary cutbacks.

I would like to thank the following contributors: Amanda Pua Walsh, Amos Clifford, Betsy Perluss, Bonnie Casamassima, Craig Chalquist, PhD, Faith Adiele, Gordon Hempton, Hobie Hare, Itzhak Beery, Janine Bendickson, Janine Benyus, Jean Shinoda Bolen, PhD, John Kiesendahl, John Perkins, Josh Heath, Julie Plevin, Kara Daniels, Kim Hermanson, PhD, Les Stroud, Lisa Kahn, Llyn Roberts, Maia Toll, Mark Setton, PhD, Nicole Craanen, Nina Simons, Oliver Heath, Patsy Balacchi, Pete Nelson, Sally Augustin, PhD, Sandra Ingerman, Sofia Batalha, Sonja Bochart, Sumita Singha, PhD, Sylvie Rokab, and Vanessa Champion, PhD.

Specifically, thanks to Gordon Hempton and Nina Simons, who not only contributed to this book but gave precious time to impart their great wisdom and help shape the final product of this book.

I also want to thank those that took the time for an interview to share their beautiful stories but did not make the final cut of the book. There are countless others, who in the process of writing unofficially shared their personal stories with me and fed my cravings for all things nature-connected. These stories may be the inspiration for a future book, podcast, or alternative storytelling medium.

Big hugs to my friends Kathleen Keenan and Kit Thomas who have seen my deeper calling to the Earth and confirm what I know to be true. And to Kathleen's midwifing of my sacred Skye experience. I hope that I can offer others such earth-shaking glimpses into their authentic selves!

So much gratitude to my book coach, Suzanne Boothby, who has guided and sustained me throughout the process of this book, and my previous one, *Creating Luminous Space* (Conari Press, 2018). Suzanne has been key to my writing process with her wisdom, humor, and her contagious enthusiasm from the sidelines!

Gratitude to my team at Mango Publishing, specifically Brenda Knight and Robin Miller, who share my vision for this book. I appreciate their knowledge, skillful support, and the sharing of their own personal stories with me.

Thanks to my colleagues at Sweetbriar Nature Center in Smithtown, NY, where I volunteer and learn how to stay connected with the local habitat and wildlife. I have become much wiser and a better steward of the land because of my deep friendships and experiences there.

Special gratitude to my sister, Pat Matheson, for being my constant cheerleader—delighting in my victories and supporting me through my challenges, just as our mother, Dorothy, would if she were here.

Speaking of my mother, I have so much gratitude for her guidance from the ether throughout this project. A few years ago, she came to me in a dream, with a message that this book would unfold and that she would be my editor from the other side. I have felt her gentle unseen hand, guiding connections with many like-minded people to reveal this book when the time was right.

And finally, I am grateful for the patience of my loving and supportive husband of nearly forty years, Joe, who continues to brighten my world with laughter and play, and reminds me of the pleasures and enchantedness of everyday life.

About the Author

A sought-after speaker, author, teacher, and consultant, Maureen Calamia is driven by her passion for the natural world.

She empowers others to discover and nourish their relationship with nature in both their inner and outer landscapes. Author of *Creating Luminous Spaces: Use the Five Elements for Balance and Harmony in Your Home and in Your Life* (Conari Press, 2018), she is a known expert in the field of feng shui.

As founder of the Luminous Spaces School since 2015, Maureen offers online courses on feng shui, biophilic design, earth healing and dowsing, mindfulness, and spirituality. She is a columnist on these topics in the *Journal of Biophilic Design* and Medium.com.

After working in the corporate world for twenty-five years, she had a dream infused with meaning that has been unfolding ever since, guiding her purpose over the last two decades. Her explorations have led her into the topics of consciousness and our connection with nature and other-than-human beings. She is a forever student, with decades of study in depth psychology, dreamwork, astrology, ecopsychology, and biophilic design.

Maureen served on the board of directors of the International Feng Shui Guild for ten years and is currently a board member and a baby squirrel caregiver at Sweetbriar Nature Center, Smithtown, New York.

Maureen is an inspirational thought leader on consciousness and being a mindful steward of the Earth through the power of reclaiming and sharing our sacred stories of nature.

Follow Maureen as she talks with her guests about their magical stories on *The Enchanted Earth Podcast*.

Youtube: www.youtube.com/@TheEnchantedEarth

Apple: podcasts.apple.com/us/podcast/the-enchanted-earth-podcast-with-maureen-calamia/id1741814139

Spotify: open.spotify.com/show/23yGA1bgFyZyv4ix2xLmde

Her website: www.luminous-spaces.com

Mango Publishing, established in 2014, publishes an eclectic list of books by diverse authors—both new and established voices—on topics ranging from business, personal growth, women's empowerment, LGBTQ+ studies, health, and spirituality to history, popular culture, time management, decluttering, lifestyle, mental wellness, aging, and sustainable living. We were named 2019 *and* 2020's #1 fastest growing independent publisher by *Publishers Weekly*. Our success is driven by our main goal, which is to publish high-quality books that will entertain readers as well as make a positive difference in their lives.

Our readers are our most important resource; we value your input, suggestions, and ideas. We'd love to hear from you—after all, we are publishing books for you!

Please stay in touch with us and follow us at:

Facebook: Mango Publishing

Twitter: @MangoPublishing

Instagram: @MangoPublishing

LinkedIn: Mango Publishing

Pinterest: Mango Publishing

Newsletter: mangopublishinggroup.com/newsletter

Join us on Mango's journey to reinvent publishing, one book at a time.

www.ingramcontent.com/pod-product-compliance
Lightning Source LLC
Chambersburg PA
CBHW011957150426
43200CB00018B/2926